The End of Prosperity

The End of Prosperity

The American Economy in the 1970s

by Harry Magdoff
and Paul M. Sweezy

Monthly Review Press
New York and London

Library of Congress Cataloging in Publication Data

Magdoff, Harry.
The end of prosperity.

Ten essays from Monthly Review magazine from May 1973 to April 1977.
1. United States—Economic conditions—1971-
—Addresses, essays, lectures. I. Sweezy, Paul Marlor,
1910- joint author. II. Title.
HC106.7.M3 330.9′73′0924 77-76168
ISBN 0-85345-422-1

First Printing

Monthly Review Press
62 West 14th Street, New York, N.Y. 10011
47 Red Lion Street, London WC1R 4 PF

Manufactured in the United States of America

Contents

Preface

The term "prosperity" is used at times in a narrow technical sense to describe the upward swing of the recurrent capitalist business cycle, without reference to long-term trends. Here we are using the word in a more general sense. By "the end of prosperity" we mean the end of the long period from the 1940s to the early 1970s during which capital accumulation on a global scale proceeded with unwonted and perhaps even unprecedented vigor. The period was characterized by what were, measured by historical standards, relatively long cyclical upswings and mild recessions. We are now several years into a new period of sluggish capital accumulation, unemployment in the advanced capitalist countries on a scale not seen since the 1930s, and rising political tensions in both the imperialist center and the colonial/neocolonial periphery of the world system. This change from prosperity to stagnation clearly marks an historic turning point of the greatest importance. Our purpose in these essays, all of which appeared in *Monthly Review* between 1973 and 1977, is to throw light on the causes of the end of prosperity and to explore, albeit unsystematically, some of its consequences and implications. Our focus is on the United States both because it is the country we know best and because it occupied a unique position as the hegemonic power in the world capitalist system during the post-Second World War period of prosperity.

—H.M., P.M.S.

New York May 1, 1977

The Dollar Crisis: What Next?

April 1973

The downfall of the Bretton Woods monetary system imposed on the capitalist world by the United States at the end of the Second World War is now complete. This system was originally based on the equivalence of gold and dollars (at $35 an ounce) as universal money to be held by member countries as monetary reserves and used as means of international payment. As long as other countries were willing to accept this basis, which was the case for more than two decades, the United States was in effect provided with a free gold mine. Golden dollars rolled off the printing press and took their place on a par with the yellow metal sweated out of the South African mines by superexploited black workers. It was a wonderful system while it lasted. Just how wonderful was graphically described to a Congressional Committee in 1965 by Robert Roosa who was at the time Undersecretary of the Treasury for Monetary Affairs. Roosa was explaining to the Committee advantages the United States would *not* have enjoyed but for this dollar/gold monetary system:

We might have been forced long ago to cut down our imports (perhaps through deflation of our economy), reduce materially our foreign investments, income from which make a substantial con-

This article originally appeared in the May 1973 issue of *Monthly Review*.

tribution to our current balance of payments, and curtail, perhaps sharply, our military and economic assistance to our friends and allies. Had we taken these steps, our customers abroad would have sharply reduced their purchases in this country and we would now be confronted with discriminatory policies against the dollar in most countries of the world. Instead of rapid growth of world trade, we would have witnessed stagnation that would have been harmful to our own prosperity and to that of the whole free world.*

The continuation of this highly privileged position naturally depended on the United States using a certain amount of restraint in resorting to the printing press. As long as paper dollars were not doled out to the rest of the world in greater amounts than the other countries needed as additional reserves and to settle international obligations, all was well. But as soon as the United States began shoveling them out at a faster rate, the basis for eventual trouble was obviously being laid. What is involved here is really nothing but the most elementary principle of monetary theory, dating back to the beginnings of modern political economy, namely, that an overissue of paper money causes it to depreciate in terms of metallic money with real value, i.e., money the amount of which can be increased only through the application of determinate amounts of human labor.

At this point we should pause and ask two questions: First, why should the United States have been issuing *any* new dollars to other countries (i.e., dollars over and above what they already held)? And second, what caused the United States to step up this outflow of dollars to a rate in excess of what the other countries needed for monetary and trade purposes?

The answer to the first question is not at all obvious, especially to anyone accustomed to thinking in terms of orthodox economics. As a leading producer of agricultural and industrial commodities, the United States had a favorable trade balance (excess of exports over imports) from well before the end of the nineteenth century right up to the 1970s. U.S. trade has thus traditionally been a source of money inflows, not outflows. Similarly, the kind of services which advanced countries provide to underdeveloped countries (shipping, insurance, etc.) are

---

* Quoted in Harry Magdoff, *The Age of Imperialism* (New York Monthly Review Press, 1969), p. 106.

money earners. And even foreign investment, though the accounts are kept in such a way as to obscure the fact, generates much more income than outgo.* And yet, beginning about 1950 the United States began to run a deficit in its balance of payments (excess of total money outflows over inflows) and except for one year has continued to do so ever since.

Why? The answer lies in government spending abroad for such purposes as putting war-torn capitalist (but not socialist) countries on their feet, military bases, limited wars, and military and economic subsidies to client states. Orthodox bourgeois social science has no way to explain expenditures of this kind except as the result of specially invented factors like the threat of "Communist aggression and subversion," the generosity of the American people to less fortunate breeds, or the application of supposedly scientific principles of economics to the elimination of poverty and underdevelopment in the Third World, all of which are of course demonstrably phoney or nonexistent. Marxists on the other hand have no difficulty in recognizing in these categories of government spending the costs of empire which normally have to be borne by the leading imperialist power or powers. We can therefore state unequivocally that the continuing post-Second World War deficit in the U.S. balance of payments is caused by the huge foreign-exchange costs of controlling a world-wide empire in the last half of the twentieth century.**

The answer to the second question—what caused the United States to step up the outflow of dollars to a rate in excess of what the other countries needed for monetary and trade purposes?—is twofold. For one thing, the costs of empire in the sense just explained were sharply inflated by the Vietnam War, the longest and second-most-costly war in U.S. history.

---

* In the 22 years 1950-1971, the Department of Commerce reported that new direct foreign capital investment outflow (by far the most important type of U.S. foreign investment) totaled $46.3 billion, while direct foreign investment income came to $88.4 billion—an excess of income over outflow of $42.1 billion or about 90 percent. *Survey of Current Business*, October 1972, pp. 26-27 (for the period 1950-1959); and June 1972, p. 26 (for the period 1960-1971).

** The *foreign-exchange* costs of empire are of course only a fraction of the *total* costs. Most of the so-called national defense budget, amounting to $75.9 billion in 1972, is spent inside the United States and hence has no direct effect on the balance of payments.

And for another thing, the U.S. trade surplus began to dwindle under the impact of domestic inflation and tougher European and Japanese competition for export markets, finally giving way to an actual trade deficit in 1971. Both of these factors began to operate in a big way around 1965, and from then on the outflow of dollars rose continuously and without any relation at all to the reserve and payments requirements of the other capitalist countries. Once this began to happen it was only a matter of time until the dollar would have to be devalued in terms of the currencies of other powerful capitalist countries with healthier balances of payments. And this time was greatly shortened by the actions of multinational corporations, speculators, and Middle East oil countries, all holders of huge amounts of dollars and able to see the handwriting on the wall. They changed big chunks of dollars into marks, yen, francs, etc., thus swelling the pressure on the dollar.

Foreign governments and central banks fought long and hard to prevent this raging dollar flood from having its natural effects in lowering the exchange value of the dollar. For example, if, as happened on various occasions, dollar holders decided that the most desirable currency was German marks, they would begin exchanging dollars for marks, thus tending to drive the price of the dollar down and of the mark up. To prevent this from happening, the German central bank would buy dollars in support of the official exchange rate. But this would involve creating a new supply of marks which could not help adding fuel to the flames of inflation in Germany, regardless of whether this was regarded by the authorities as good or bad for the health of the German economy. In the long run, of course, it was a losing battle: the other countries couldn't go on forever buying up all the dollars pouring out of the United States and into their own central banks; and the clearer it became that the end was approaching, the greater became the pressure on the dollar-exchange rate, as more dollar holders hurried to get into other currencies while the getting was still good.

The first principle of the Bretton Woods system to be abandoned was the convertibility of the dollar into gold. This occurred *de facto* in March 1968 and *de jure* in August 1971. Between these dates a number of devaluations (e.g., the pound and the French franc) and revaluations (e.g., the German mark) took place, but on the whole the Bretton Woods system of fixed exchange rates, though badly battered, still stood. It collapsed beyond repair, however, with the official abandonment of gold convertibility by the United States on August 15, 1971. By that time the dollars held abroad amounted to $53.3 billion (as against only $10.5 billion gold in U.S. reserves). A last effort was made to put Humpty Dumpty back together again in the form of the Smithsonian agreement of December 1971, which officially devalued the dollar and set up a new supposedly fixed schedule of rates among the various currencies of the participating countries. Nixon hailed this as the most important monetary agreement in the history of the world, but it didn't help. Dollars kept on pouring out until by early 1973 there were some $82 billion of them held outside the United States.* A number of incidents, some apparently quite trivial, triggered a fresh international monetary crisis in February and March of this year, and it soon became clear that the power of governments and central banks to calm it down through traditional means had finally run out. The dollar was this time officially devalued overnight, but this was little more than a hollow gesture, since in fact all pretense at fixed exchange rates had to be simultaneously abandoned. The truth is that there is no longer anything that can properly be called an international monetary system: there are just a collection of national currencies which relate to each other on a day-to-day basis in response to a variety of economic, political, and psychological forces.

Many economists, including some of the most prestigious, regard this as a good thing. They argue that under the old system speculation against the dollar (for example, by buying marks or yen) was pretty close to a sure thing. If the mark or the yen should eventually be pushed up, the speculators could return to dollars with more than they had at the outset. But

* Even this enormous sum understates the amount of liquid resources sloshing around in the world and available for transfer from one country to another. The *Wall Street Journal* of February 13, 1973, reporting on a study of multinational corporations by the U.S. Tariff Commission, states: "The study estimates that some $268 billion of short-term liquid assets were held at the end of 1971 by 'private institutions on the international financial scene,' and that the 'lion's share' of the money was controlled by U.S.-based multinational companies and banks."

even if the existing parities should hold, the worst that could happen to them would be a standoff. It's like making a bet which you might win but can't lose, something every gambler dreams of. Under the new circumstances, the reasoning is, with all currencies floating the risk of loss is increased to balance the chance of gain (since all currencies can now move up or down with equal ease). This, the economists think, should serve greatly to reduce the amount of speculation and should therefore permit all currencies to find their "true" values, i.e., the values determined by underlying balance-of-payments realities.

The trouble with this theory is that it is purely formal and neglects to take account of what those underlying realities are. We know that what ruined the Bretton Woods system was a persistent and growing deficit in the U.S. balance of payments which poured dollars out on the rest of the world into a swelling reservoir. The sources of this deficit were the costs of empire and (since 1971) an unfavorable balance of trade. The question is: Are there any signs that either of these sources is being dammed up or eliminated?

The answer, of course, is none whatever. For a time it seemed that the Nixon administration had at least decided to cut out that part of the costs of empire stemming from the war in Indochina; but with the latest news from Cambodia even this now seems doubtful, and in any case it would only somewhat reduce the dollar outflow on this account. As far as the trade deficit is concerned, it reached a new high of $6.8 billion in 1972 and shows no sign of declining. In other words, the dollar hemorrhage continues and may even be growing. Apart from day-to-day fluctuations, how can this help but drive the dollar further down? And if this is indeed the real situation, isn't speculation against the dollar just about as sure a thing as it was before?

What all this adds up to is that under the new regime of floating currencies the prospect is for a continuing and very likely accelerating decline in the international value of the dollar. And this means what the more serious bourgeois ideologists and analysts know in their hearts but shrink from saying aloud, that U.S. capitalism and hence also the world capitalist system is headed for an unprecedented crisis.

There is not much point, however, in elaborating on the precise nature of the crisis which lies at the end of the road that is now being traveled—if only because it is certain that strenuous efforts are going to be made to pull back and divert events into other channels. And these efforts, whether or not successful in achieving their intended results, will change the givens of the problem. This is not to argue that we are not headed for a crisis (or series of crises), but only that it will not be the simple logical outcome of the progressive devaluation of the dollar. All we need to do, therefore, is to indicate why the U.S. bourgeoisie cannot sit by and watch the dollar go down the drain.

Basically, the reason is that the other side of the devaluation coin is domestic inflation, and the more devaluation the more inflation. Pushed to its furthest limits, the outcome could only be hyperinflation with drastically disruptive social effects domestically and virtual impotence internationally.* Since the

* Orthodox static theory would tend to argue that the devaluation process is fundamentally self-correcting. As the dollar sinks, exports (now cheaper in terms of foreign currencies) increase, and imports (more expensive for domestic buyers) decline. In this way a trade deficit is supposed to be turned into a surplus and the surplus eventually to grow large enough to restore equilibrium to the balance of payments, at which point the devaluation process comes to an end. Historically, however, there is little evidence of such an equilibrating mechanism and much reason to believe that devaluations normally set in train cumulative processes which lead away from rather than toward equilibrium. In the U.S. case, for example, the cheapening of exports for foreigners, especially agricultural products which are an important component of U.S. exports, may reduce domestic supplies and send internal prices zooming up (this indeed seems to be a part of the explanation of the present skyrocketing food prices in this country), and any increase in prices in one sector of the economy tends to spread to others. On the import side, a large part of what the United States buys from abroad is necessary for the functioning of the economy and hence quite insensitive to price changes. When the dollar price of such commodities (many raw materials increasingly including oil and natural gas, tropical products, etc.) rises, the effect is to spur the outflow of dollars, perhaps more than offsetting the savings on other more price-sensitive imports. Furthermore—and this is often overlooked in discussions of the subject—in a regime of monopoly capitalism the prices of all commodities which are internationally traded, *whether or not they figure in U.S. exports or imports,* tend to be rapidly adjusted to the world price level which, measured in dollars, of course rises as the devaluation process progresses. All in all, there would seem to be no reason for the United States (or anyone else except an orthodox economist) to count on devaluation to restore equilibrium to its balance of payments and thus to arrest the devaluation process.

American ruling class is obviously not likely to acquiesce in such a prospect, the real question to be answered is what other options are open to it.

The most logical one, at least as a first step and as an earnest of a sincere desire to change the situation, would be substantially to reduce the costs of empire—liquidating the war in Indochina, closing foreign bases, bringing home troops, leaving repressive and unpopular regimes in many countries to be dealt with by their own people, etc. It is perfectly clear, however, that the Nixon administration has no intention of moving in this direction and more likely intends to act in ways which will increase the costs of empire. Under these circumstances, it has no choice but to attempt to operate on the balance of payments through the private sector, which means (1) by improving the balance of trade, and (2) by increasing the net take from foreign investment. Let us review the possibilities under both these heads.

Balance of Trade. Improving the balance of trade means some combination of reducing imports and increasing exports. In textbook economics, devaluation of a country's currency is supposed to do both automatically; but as we have already argued, this has not happened in the U.S. case in the last two years and historical experience provides no evidence that it will accomplish anything sensational in the future.* More active measures are therefore called for.

As newspaper readers know, it is the fashion in political and financial circles to talk about solving all these problems—monetary as well as trade—through "negotiations" with the other advanced capitalist countries. But it is doubtful if any one who is familiar with the realities takes this talk seriously. What the United States wants is that its imports (their exports)

---

* An article in the *Wall Street Journal* (February 5, 1973) entitled "Do Devaluations Really Help Trade?", by Arthur B. Laffer of the University of Chicago Business School, argues, with interesting supporting data, that while there is little evidence of a close correlation between exchange rates and trade balances, there is strong reason to believe that a country's trade balance is negatively correlated with the relative rate of growth of its GNP. This would point to deliberate deflation as the policy most likely to improve the balance of payments. While the Nixon administration, in common with many bankers and conservative economists, might prefer this course on ideological grounds, the political risks are obviously too great to make it a realistic option.

should be reduced, and its exports (their imports) should be increased. But the other countries want the same thing in reverse, and it is obvious that they are not going to hand over to the United States what it wants on a silver platter; that would be not negotiation but simple surrender. There was a time when the United States was strong enough to impose its own solution —and the result was the Bretton Woods system with all its accompanying benefits. But nothing proves more conclusively than the collapse of that system that U.S. strength has turned into U.S. weakness. This doesn't mean that there will be no negotiations, only that all parties concerned will be looking out for their own interests, with no guarantee that the United States will get more than it gives and no chance whatever that it will win the sweeping concessions which would be necessary to restore the dollar to health.

In the jungle world of capitalism if you can't get what you want by negotiating from a position of strength, the next step is to consider forcing the issue. You won't do it of course if you're pretty sure it won't work. But if you think there's a reasonable chance and if you're a bold fellow, you'll go right ahead. That's where the Nixon administration is now in the arena of international economic relations. Under cover of preparing for negotiations it is actually preparing for economic warfare. And it isn't even trying to keep it a secret. "I think," *Business Week* (February 17) quotes a government trade official as saying, "the administration has made up its mind to start a trade war if necessary."

Actually, this is an understatement: the administration has already started a trade war. In the words of Richard B. Du Boff:

> Future trade negotiations, and international commerce in general, are headed into stormy seas. It would not be far-fetched to assert that a four-cornered trade war, among the United States, Canada, Japan, and the EEC, has begun.
>
> Though public awareness of it seems scant, the Nixon administration began mounting a coordinated campaign of harassment against its major trading partners a year ago. ("The Devalued Dollar," *Commonweal,* March 30, 1973, p. 81)

Du Boff proceeds to support these statements with numerous specific cases centering on the use of existing anti-dumping legislation. These, however, were only preliminary skirmishes and, as the widening 1972 trade deficit shows, were failing to produce significant results. "On August 31, 1972," Du Boff reports, "a high administration source quoted the exasperated President as feeling that 'our trading partners are turning out to be our trading competitors. . . . We can withstand a trade war better than any other country in the world.' The source added that 'the President's patience has run out.' " During the fall and winter months, Nixon was preoccupied with getting out of Vietnam on the best (from his point of view) terms obtainable, a sort of partial clearing of the decks for the larger struggle to come. By spring he was ready for the next step in the form of a comprehensive new trade bill, which he sent to the Congress on April 10th.

On the face of it, as well as in Nixon's accompanying message, this bill is aimed at liberalizing the world's trading system, the theory being that an all-around reduction in barriers to trade would lead to a big expansion of U.S. exports. The bill therefore would give Nixon very wide powers to increase and/or to reduce tariff and nontariff obstacles to trade, powers which he could presumably use to good effect in bargaining with other countries. All of this, however, is really beside the point for two reasons. First, as already suggested above, there is no reason to suppose that the United States could negotiate changes in trading relations which would increase its exports substantially more than its imports. And second, it is quite likely that the reason U.S. exports have suffered relative to those of the other advanced capitalist countries has a good deal less to do with trade barriers than with such factors as marketing skills, quality of goods, and the build-up by U.S.-based multinational corporations of overseas production facilities. The liberalization-through-bargaining route, in short, holds out no prospect of a significant turnaround in the U.S. trade balance.

This does not mean, however, that the bill lacks teeth. In this connection what has to be kept in mind is that while the United States (or any other country) may find it difficult or even impossible to influence the volume of its exports, the same is definitely not true of its imports. And when it is further remembered that the deterioration in the U.S. trade balance in recent years has been due to a much more rapid growth of imports than of exports (in the five-year period 1968-1972, imports increased by 69 percent, exports by 45 percent), the meaning of the proposed trade bill can be seen in its true light. Here, as summarized by the *New York Times* (April 11), are two of its key provisions:

- The President would have new powers to impose import restrictions on goods from countries engaging in such unfair trade practices as putting limitations on goods from the United States or subsidizing their own exports.
- There would be wholly new authority for the President to impose sweeping import taxes or quotas in case of serious deficits in the nation's balance of international payments, and to reduce all or most tariffs in the opposite situation—a major surplus in the United States balance of payments.

Armed with these powers, Nixon could overnight eliminate the trade deficit, and from what we know of the man it is a pretty good guess that this is precisely what he would do. But the aggrieved "partners," especially Japan and the Common Market, could hardly take a blow like that lying down, which is the reason for believing that what has so far been preliminary skirmishing is on the way to becoming full-scale warfare.

Foreign Investment. At the time of the latest dollar devaluation, Treasury Secretary Shultz announced that the administration intends to seek the elimination of all controls on capital outflow by December 31, 1974. On the face of it this seems incongruous, to say the least, as part of a program designed to improve the country's balance of payments. Robert Roosa, now a partner in the investment banking firm of Brown Brothers Harriman, speaking at a dinner meeting of the Economic Club of New York on March 14th, called it a "gratuitous commitment"; and from the opposite end of the ideological spectrum comes Richard Du Boff's statement (in the article quoted above) that "elimination of all capital controls . . . is a hazardous step for a nation with a balance of payments deficit since it could trigger further outflows of private capital—but it provides eloquent testimony to Nixon's real priorities." Neither analyst, however, gives any indication of why the Nixon administration should be taking this occasion to call attention to its determination to eliminate these (not very strict) capital controls.

The most plausible explanation would seem to be that the administration is in full agreement with the country's giant multinational corporations that in the long run the best hope for the balance of payments and hence for the restoration of a strong dollar lies in the maximum possible increase in the income from foreign direct investment.* By announcing its intention to end capital controls—at a time when a more obvious move would have been to *strengthen* these controls—Nixon is signalling to the multinationals that they should keep right on expanding their foreign operations with the assurance of government approval and support. The risks of adverse short-term balance-of-payments effects are apparently not considered too great, which may be explained by the fact that most multinationals are now in a position to finance foreign expansion not through exporting capital but through reinvesting foreign profits and tapping local money markets.

If we are right, the Nixon administration is counting on two strategies to reverse the continuing and ultimately disastrous deterioration of the dollar: an extremely aggressive trade policy involving bitter economic warfare on the one hand, and an expansion of the income from foreign investments on the other. What now needs to be added is that these two strategies are interrelated in a contradictory way.

Economic warfare, once it breaks out into the open, cannot and will not be confined to the field of trade. It will spread to encompass the entire gamut of international relations. Every country will perforce apply increasingly strict controls over foreign exchange rates, movements of capital, repatriation of profits. And the freedom of multinational corporations to do what they like with their assets and their profits will be progressively restricted. The multinational corporation's idea of utopia has been "one world" with a sovereign federal government, uniform laws, a single currency, and absolute freedom to operate where

* For a detailed discussion of the logic of this position, see "Balance of Payments and Empire," *Monthly Review,* December 1972.

they want and move when they want. The real world has never been quite like that of course, but it never approached this condition so closely as during the heyday of U.S. hegemony in the 1950s and 1960s. Now, with that hegemony a thing of the past, the monetary system in disarray, and a shattering trade war in the offing, the multinational corporation is going to have to abandon this dream and adjust to a very different reality.

The full implications of this change will probably not be clear for a long time to come. But even at this stage it seems safe to predict that in conditions of open economic warfare the position of the U.S. multinationals will become a difficult one. As already indicated, the U.S. government sees in them a crucially important instrument in righting the balance of payments and thus checking the declining power of U.S. capitalism. On the other hand, most of them will be functioning to a significant extent in jurisdictions which are being attacked by U.S. trade and related policies. If in these circumstances they play the role assigned to them by their own government, expanding their operations and transferring more and more profits to the United States, they will come under growing pressure from the governments of the host countries, egged on by rival capitalists anxious to seize a larger share of local markets.

There would seem to be no way out of this dilemma. If they play as loyal members of the U.S. team, they will be subject to retaliation, which might take many forms, all the way from the embargoing of profit transfers to full nationalization (which in any case is a tempting way for a number of countries to unload unwanted excess dollars). And if they decide that the better part of wisdom is to act like good citizens of the host countries, they can hardly at the same time perform the function of transferring wealth on a massive scale to the mother country. Probably sooner rather than later, the Nixon strategists will discover that it is impossible to wage economic warfare and at the same time enjoy the fruits of peaceful economic penetration.

When this times comes, the U.S. ruling class will have to seek other strategies to check the decline of American capitalism. They are likely to encompass the imposition of tight controls on the whole economy and society, involving a sharp increase in the domestic rate of surplus value; the formation, by military means if necessary, of a dollar bloc run from Washington, embracing at a minimum all of North and Central America; severe competition with other imperialist metropolises for dominance in Asia, South America, Africa, and the Middle East; possibly joint action, once again including military means, with these other metropolises to bring the oil exporting countries to heel; and the courting of the political, economic, and, if need be, military support of the noncapitalist countries against rival imperialisms and the world revolution. The United States has already begun to move in some of these directions, but it seems doubtful whether it can go much further unless or until basic changes have been effected in the organization and exercise of political power within the country. The period ahead, short-term and long-term alike, promises to be characterized by unprecedented upheavals, explosions, and struggles on the internal as well as the international scene.

A Note on Inflation

December 1973

Inflation is a possibility in any society that uses money as a medium of exchange, but it is an inescapable and distinguishing feature of capitalism—and most especially in its monopoly stage. From their beginnings, and throughout their long history, capitalist countries have at times been plagued and at other times stimulated by bursts of inflation. In essence, these recurring waves are both symptom and cause of the instability inherent in the anarchic production system of capitalism. It is true that especially severe inflationary episodes have resulted from currency mismanagement by governments and banks. And even more severe currency depreciations have been caused by armaments races, wars, and the aftermath of wars. But the distortions created by these special progenitors of inflation—currency manipulation and wars—are themselves either products of, or means adopted to cope with, the unremitting instability of capitalism.

Whatever the immediate causes of inflation may be—and without taking into account the inflation-induced contradictions which are resolved by economic depressions—rapid price rises produce two important results for a capitalist society. First, they act as a stimulus to investment. This is especially the case when price advances are persistent and do not spiral too quickly.

This is the text of a reply by Harry Magdoff to a request for a brief statement on inflation from the editors of the Mexican journal *Problemas del Desarrollo*: *Revista Latinoamericana de Economía*. It originally appeared in the December 1973 issue of *Monthly Review*.

Under such circumstances, speculative fever is rife, the urge to accumulate inventory is strong, and the environment is favorable for new risk-taking by entrepreneurs. Second, inflation serves to redistribute income in favor of some sectors of the population and to the disadvantage of others. Typically, it is an instrument for the protection and expansion of surplus value, i.e., the share of the national product appropriated by the capitalists. The propensity to start and feed the flames of an inflationary spiral grows naturally out of a society that is guided by the profit motive. Since it is the duty and destiny of each capitalist enterprise to increase its profits, every practical device for this purpose is seized upon, whether it takes the form of reducing costs of production or raising the price of the finished product. The capitalist is hence always on the lookout for ways to raise his prices. The price-raising path to higher profits is, however, restricted when competition among capitalists is widespread. On the other hand, the inflationary tendency begins to take over as the force of competition diminishes.

The relevance of inflation in capitalism is best understood against the background of historical changes in the structure of this socioeconomic order. Infant capitalism was rooted in rampant inflation, the latter spurred by the commercial revolution, the looting of the treasures of colonial acquisitions, and the flood of cheap gold and silver obtained with forced labor from the mines of Latin America. Although long upward waves of prices were followed by prolonged deflations (tied up with alternating periods of prosperity and stagnation and often associated with the successes and failures of colonial exploitation), the dominant and most influential trend during the centuries of evolution of merchant capitalism was inflation.

Quite the opposite is the case as capitalism moved from the commercial to the industrial phase. Declining commodity prices not only became a characteristic phenomenon, but were in fact elements contributing to economic success, instead of, as in the past, accompaniments of stagnation. Reductions in production costs achieved in the age of machinery were reflected in long-run price declines, under the impetus of competition. When there were many relatively small firms in each industry, among which collusion was difficult or impossible, businessmen were forced to fight each other by cutting prices, where cost savings permitted. The common method of increasing profits was to capture the markets of competitors by underselling them. Even under these conditions, wars and cyclical booms created waves of inflation, but these were overtaken eventually by relatively long periods of declining prices, made possible and necessary by technical advance and competition.

This type of price behavior changed dramatically when concentration and centralization of capital reached the point where direct and indirect collusion and control of markets by relatively few giant firms in each industry became the rule. With the appearance of monopoly capitalism, a secular trend of inflation set in. Cyclical depressions at times produced a downward adjustment of prices. In addition, war-induced hyper-inflations often led to major price corrections. But the innate tendency of capitalism toward inflation became dominant as soon as monopolistic-type control spread throughout the industrial system.

The contrasting behavior of prices in the stages of competitive and monopoly capitalism can be observed in the following two tables, which summarize the major trends in U.S. wholesale prices during the past 150 years. First let us look at the earliest 75 years of this time span, from 1823 to 1898, a period that covers the inception and maturation of competitive capitalism in the United States.

TABLE I

U.S. Wholesale Price Index
(1823=100)

Year	Index
1823	100
1848	75
1873	139
1898	74

Source: *Hearings before the Joint Economic Committee on Employment, Growth, and Price Levels, Part 2* (Washington, D.C.: U.S. Govt. Printing Office, 1959), pp. 395-396.

As can be seen, the net wholesale price change in the United States between 1823 and 1898 was downward. In the interim there was a wild cyclical price swing due to the huge volume of paper currency issued by the U.S. government to finance the Civil War. This war-induced inflation was followed by a long period of deflation, with wholesale prices getting back to pre-Civil War levels in the 1880s. Thus, the height of the wholesale price index shown above for 1873 still reflects the impact of the induced inflation associated with the Civil War and its aftermath. Given the eventual return of conservative monetary practices, the downward price pressure of competitive capitalism reasserted itself. By 1898, when monopoly capitalism was already blossoming and affecting price practices, the wholesale price index was roughly the same as that of 50 years earlier. Now note how very different the experience of the past 75 years has been.

TABLE 2

U U.S. Wholesale Price Index

(1898=100)

1898	100
1923	208
1948	331
1973 (first 8 months)	530

Sources: 1898 to 1948: same as Table 1; 1948 to 1973: *Emonomic Indicator* (Washington, D.C.: U.S. Government Printing Office, various monthly issues). The price indexes were spliced and converted to an 1898 base.

These data suggest that the present inflationary process is not at all a new phenomenon. While the rates of price increase have recently been accelerating and while this acceleration may be an omen of an approaching new hyperinflation, it is nevertheless important to recognize the consistency of the secular inflationary trend over the past three-quarters of a century. The year-to-year changes over this long period have been far from regular: each big war contributed to the hyperinflation of some currencies in the advanced capitalist nations; in addition, the great depression of the 1930s lowered price levels throughout the capitalist world. But despite erratic and cyclical year-to-year movements, the inflationary trend always reasserted itself; at the end of each 25-year interval summarized in Table 2, the price level reached a new high.

Usually when one finds such a persistent trend in economic behavior, it is the result of more than one simple cause. Here too the contributing factors are many. But what is significant is that the multi-faceted and mutually reinforcing promoters of inflation are all related in varying degrees to the nature and structure of monopoly capitalism. The following are some of these:

(1) The new imperialism of this stage of capitalism stimulates the growth of armaments and the spread of wars.

(2) The tendency, however reluctant, on the part of powerful sectors of the capitalist class to grant wage concessions to sections of the working class in the hope of getting popular support for imperialist wars and policies.

(3) The widespread use of protective tariffs and other trade barriers as weapons of commercial warfare.

(4) The greater integration of the world capitalist system, resulting in the spread of inflation from one country to another.

(5) The growth of large-scale banking and credit expansion as financial instruments for the spread of giant corporations. With this comes the larger use of credit and the pumping up of the money supply. (For an explanation of the expanding credit system and its role, see Thorstein Veblen, *Absentee Ownership* [New York: Huebsch, 1923], chapter 12.)

(6) With the possibility of controlling large segments of the market, the giant corporations compete for market shares by manipulating consumers through advertising, other means of sales promotion, and fostering consumer credit—leading to higher costs and higher prices in times of prosperity and to resistance to price declines in depressions.

(7) The tendency to economic stagnation characteristic of monopoly capitalism induces greater economic activity by the state. This takes various forms, including money manipulations and government spending designed to create a favorable (i.e., inflationary) environment for business.

While all these factors have in one way or another played a role in furthering the inflation of the post-Second World War period, it appears that the last item (point 7) has been the most important contributor to present ills. The manipulators of government finance suffer from the illusion that they can regulate the economy to obtain an even and moderate pace of price increases. But the truth is that such "fine-tuning" is not feasible amidst the contradictory economic pressures and the very distortions that inflation induces. The experience of recent decades supplies ample evidence that the inflationary techniques used to stimulate the economy artificially neither resolve the contradictions of monopoly capitalism nor basically reverse the underlying tendency to stagnation. In fact, the very methods used to moderate business slumps and create jobs help engender new distortions and imbalances, which in turn call for ever more inflationary measures and make the entire economy addicted to these stimulants.

Disturbances in the international monetary system have been adding still another dimension to the problem. Built into the Bretton Woods system was the contradiction between its goals of stabilizing foreign exchange rates and maintaining the imperialist system. The burdens of financing imperialist control, by war and other means, eventually nullified the exchange rate stability. The breakdown of the Bretton Woods system, coming on top of the huge pile-up of U.S. dollars abroad, fostered enormous and rapid shifts of currencies among the leading capitalist powers. Such shifts, and the defensive measures taken to counter their effects (notably, support of unusually high interest rates concurrently with accelerated inflation), have played havoc with prevailing fantasies about the possibility of keeping inflation within reasonable limits.

As the inflation-induced distortions became more evident and appeared to be getting out of control, the ruling circles in the advanced capitalist nations have been turning to the problem of moderating instead of generating inflation. But the hard fact is that in a capitalist society the correction of a long stretch of inflation, and especially one that threatens to become hyperinflation, can only take the form of economic depression. Short of such a radical readjustment, temporary alleviating measures are merely means of shifting the burdens of inflation from one class or stratum to others. In a bourgeois society, this obviously means protecting business profits at the expense of the working class. The extent to which the ruling class can accomplish this depends on the vigor with which the workers pursue the class struggle. In the final analysis, however, the only defense the working class has against the alternative evils of inflation and depression is the abolition of the capitalist social system.

Keynesian Chickens Come Home to Roost

March 1974

As we have argued many times in these pages, the monopoly capitalist economy is always in danger of sinking into a state of deep stagnation. The basic reason is that capitalists seek to keep the wages and hence the purchasing power of workers at a minimum, while expanding their capital as rapidly as possible. It follows, in Marx's words, that

> to the extent that the productive power develops, it finds itself at variance with the narrow basis on which the condition of consumption rests. On this self-contradictory basis it is no contradiction at all that there should be an excess of capital simultaneously with an excess of population. For while a combination of these two would increase the mass of the produced surplus value, it would at the same time intensify the contradiction between the conditions under which this surplus value is produced and those under which it is realized. (*Capital,* Kerr ed., vol. 3, p. 287)

This source of stagnation ("excess of capital" and "excess of population"=idle plant and unemployed workers) is inherent in capitalism in all stages of its development, but it is vastly intensified in the monopoly stage because of the enormous power of giant corporations to control prices and wages in their own favor. Furthermore, in the monopoly stage consumers are regularly fleeced (for the second time in the case of workers) in the sphere of circulation by monopolistic middlemen, retailers, usurers, racketeers, etc. The result is further to reduce social

This article originally appeared in the April 1974 issue of *Monthly Review.*

consuming power and to concentrate additional income in the hands of those whose modes of expenditure are luxury consumption goods and increased capital investment. The whole system is rigged in favor of the haves and against the have-nots. The only trouble is that the more it works that way, the worse it works.

There have to be counteracting forces, and there are: otherwise the whole system would have gone down the drain long ago. On the one hand there must be massive injections of purchasing power to supplement the restricted consumption generated by the normal workings of the system; and on the other hand there must be continuously maintained incentives, chiefly in the form of a steadily rising price level, for the rich minority to invest their lavish incomes. Like a leaking tire, the economy must be unflaggingly pumped up if it is not to go flat and come to a full stop.

The simple leaking tire analogy, however, fails in one respect. As long as the economy is pumped up enough to keep going, all the monopolistic forces within it work overtime to increase their share of the take. This means higher prices, higher rates, higher fees, higher costs all along the line. And this perpetual scramble for more on the part of the powerful and the privileged exacerbates the underlying disproportions which are at the root of the system's malfunctioning. To complete our analogy we would have to say that both the tire and the leak grow with the passage of time, thus requiring a continuously larger and more active pump.

This, we believe, is the embryo of an adequate theory of inflation under conditions of monopoly capitalism. Of all the directions in which it can be elaborated and developed, we would like in what follows to focus attention on the pump—or rather on the various pumping mechanisms which work together to keep the tire from going flat. After having a look at the most important of these mechanisms, we shall present a few data to show how extraordinarily active they have become in the last few years.

The three most important pumping mechanisms can be identified under the following headings: (1) the credit system, (2) government finances, and (3) the central bank (Federal

Reserve System). They are of course closely interrelated and to a degree overlapping.

The credit system, which could equally well be called the debt system since credit and debt are two sides of the same coin, includes commercial and savings banks, various kinds of lending companies, the credit departments of industrial and retail corporations, loan sharks, and miscellaneous other agencies and institutions. To oversimplify the matter somewhat, what the credit system does is to borrow money at one rate of interest from people who have more money than they need and lend it at a much higher rate to those who need (or think they need) more than they have. In this way money is kept circulating—and debts keep mounting. We will return presently to some quantitative aspects of the matter.

In principle, government finances can operate either to inflate or deflate the economy. In practice, they almost always operate as an inflator. The hallmark of sovereignty, Veblen once remarked, is the right to make war. He might have added a second, the right to create money. If a sovereign government, like ours, spends more than it takes in, it can either print up money to cover the difference or, as is more usual under modern conditions, borrow what it needs from the banks. This might mean that in order to lend to the government the banks would have to lend less to private borrowers. But it usually doesn't, the reason being that the ability of banks to lend depends on the amount of their reserves (deposits at the central bank), and these can be varied by central bank policy. The central bank, which, whatever its juridical form, is really as much a branch of the government as the treasury, is not likely to make it hard for the banks to lend money to the government to finance its deficits, so the result is usually an injection of additional purchasing power into the system more or less commensurate with the size of the deficits.

Finally, the central bank can increase the reserves and hence the lending power of the banks quite apart from government deficits.* The determinants of central bank policy in this regard

* This is accomplished for the most part through what are called open market operations, which means purchases by the central bank of government bonds or notes on the open market. Whoever sells these securi-

are quite complex and need not concern us here. Suffice it to say that the normal bias is toward an expansionary policy. Any sign of financial trouble, as after the Penn Central bankruptcy in 1970, or a threatened increase in the unemployment rate, which as we have seen is never further away than around the next corner, generates pressure on the central bank to shoot more money into the system. There being few pressures in the opposite direction—apart from the admonitions of conservative economists—the normal outcome is a foregone conclusion.

Now that we have surveyed the pumping mechanisms, let us put together a few figures indicating the extent to which they have been operating in the latest period.

First, selected data on the growth of debt, which reflects the pumping activity of the credit system. Table 1 shows the growth of commercial bank loans since 1965. Here we see that the

TABLE I

Commercial Bank Loans

End of Year	*Billions of $*	*Percent Increase*	
1965	198.2	—	
1966	213.9	8.1	
1967	231.3	8.1	avg. 9.0
1968	258.2	11.6	
1969	279.1	8.1	
1970	291.7	4.5	
1971	320.3	9.8	
1972	377.8	18.0	avg. 15.2
1973	444.5	17.7	

Source: *The Economic Report of the President,* February 1974, p. 31.

average rate of increase of bank loans during the upswing of the early '70s (1971-1973) was almost 70 percent higher (15.2 percent as against 9.0 percent) than in the Vietnam War boom years (1965-1969).

Second, take consumer installment credit, always an important factor in the demand for consumer durable goods. Table 2 shows net annual increases in consumer installment credit

---

ties to the central bank, whether a commercial bank or a corporation or a private individual, receives a check on the Federal Reserve Bank. When these checks are deposited, they swell the banks' reserves and hence lending capacity.

TABLE 2
Net Annual Increases in Consumer Installment Credit

	Billions of Current $	*Billions of 1967 $*
1965	8.2	8.7
1966	5.3	5.5
1967	3.2	3.2
1968	8.3	8.0
1969	9.4	8.6
1970	5.0	4.3
1971	9.2	7.6
1972	16.0	12.8
1973	20.8	15.6

Source: *Ibid.*, p. 320.

since 1965. What is especially noteworthy here—but seems not to have been much noted by commentators on the current economic situation—is the way this series took off during the last two years: even allowing for inflation (i.e., measuring in constant 1967 dollars), additions to installment credit in 1972-1973 ran at around double the rate of the preceding years. This was doubtless an important factor in maintaining the demand for consumer durables (especially automobiles) during the latest cyclical upswing. By the same token, the need for especially heavy repayments during the next couple of years will exercise a depressing effect on consumer demand, quite apart from other factors such as increased unemployment and the energy-crisis-related decline in the demand for automobiles.*

Finally, mortgage debt, which in the aggregate is much larger than all other types of consumer credit put together. It used to be that most mortgage debt was incurred in order to build new housing, but in recent years more and more people have been mortgaging or re-mortgaging their homes to acquire money for other purposes. Table 3 (p. 26) goes back to 1961 to illustrate this trend more clearly.

---

* Another development in the consumer-credit area, no doubt in considerable part caused by the rapid growth of the last two years, has been a sharp rise in the delinquency rate. "The number of persons not paying their installment loans on time increased by 19 percent in November and December," begins a first-page story in the *New York Times* of February 16th.

TABLE 3

Net New Mortgage Debt and Its Uses

(Billions of dollars)

	Net New Mortgage Debt (1)	*Outlays for New Homes* (2)	*Other Uses of Mortgage Debt* (3)
		(Column 3 = 1 minus 2)	
1961	21.0	17.4	3.6
1962	23.8	19.1	4.7
1963	27.1	18.7	8.4
1964	29.4	19.1	10.3
1965	29.8	19.0	9.9
1966	28.5	18.6	9.9
1967	27.5	15.8	11.7
1968	33.2	20.8	12.4
1969	35.6	21.2	14.4
1970	32.1	18.1	14.0
1971	44.8	26.6	18.2
1972	59.8	35.6	24.2
1973 (first half)	62.8	41.1	21.8

Data are for 1-4 family houses, as estimated by the Conference Board. The data in column (1) are estimates of the flow of new mortgage money made available to consumers each year. They therefore differ from the Federal Reserve Board series which measures only mortgage debt outstanding.

Source: *The Conference Board Statistical Bulletin,* November 1973.

From our present point of view the most important thing about this table is the sensational jump in the rate of increase in mortgage debt formation since the relatively depressed year 1970 (the additional debt formed in the first half of 1973 was running at an annual rate nearly double that of 1970). No doubt whatever that this part of the credit system was pumping at or near full capacity. The table also shows clearly the trend to greater non-housing uses of mortgage debt. It is interesting that this item now runs consistently ahead of the increase in installment credit (Table 2 above). In other words, quite apart from new housing, borrowing on real estate has become the largest source of consumer debt financing. It seems that as old mortgages are paid off and real estate values rise, people find it necessary or cannot resist the temptation (and/or the blandishments of banks eager for additional business) to step up their "buy now, pay later" way of life.

We turn now to the pumping mechanism labeled "government finances." It is of course a commonplace that deficits are the rule rather than the exception nowadays; it remains only to give the notion a bit more quantitative definiteness. One way is to divide the post-Second World War period into four periods and observe the changing ratio of deficit to surplus years. In the decade 1945-1954 there were five deficit years and five of surplus (including one year of a balanced budget). In the next decade, 1955-1964, there were seven deficit years and three surplus. And in the nine years, 1965-1973, there were eight deficits and one surplus. But even more striking is the way the size of the deficits has been growing. Table 4 shows the deficits from 1965 to the present. Taking into account that 1968 was the peak year of U.S. military involvement in Southeast Asia (more than half a million troops in the region that year), one need only glance at the table to see what has been happening; and even including 1968, the cumulative deficit of the first four years of the 1970s was more than 80 percent greater than the cumulative deficit of the last four years of the 1960s. No mistaking the fact that this pumping mechanism too has been very busy these last few years!

TABLE 4

Balance of Federal Receipts and Outlays

(Billions of dollars)

(Plus=Surplus, Minus=Deficit)

Fiscal years	
1965	—1.6
1966	—3.8
1967	—8.7
1968	—25.2
1969	+3.2
1970	—2.8
1971	—23.0
1972	—23.2
1973	—14.3

Source: *The Economic Report of the President,* February 1974, p. 123.

Finally, we come to the role of the central bank in expanding the money supply. Table 5 (p. 28) shows the growth of the total money supply since 1965. (Total money supply consists of currency in circulation plus demand and time deposits at commercial banks plus deposits at non-bank thrift institutions.) The huge rates of increase attained in 1971 and 1972 were cut back

TABLE 5
Growth of the Money Supply

	Billions of $	*Percentage Increase*
1965	463	—
1966	485	4.8
1967	533	9.9
1968	577	8.3
1969	594	3.0
1970	641	7.9
1971	727	13.4
1972	822	13.1
1973	893	8.6

Source: *Ibid,* p. 310.

in 1973, but, even so, only to approximately the rate which characterized the years of peak involvement in the Vietnam war. As in the case of the other pumping mechanisms reviewed, this one seems to have reached an altogether new and higher level of activity during the 1970s.

With all the pumps going full tilt and prices rising at an accelerating rate, you might at least expect that this most recent period would have been one of relatively full utilization of labor and manufacturing capacity. But if you had this expectation, you would be mistaken. Our last table (Table 6) shows the unemployment rate and the manufacturing capacity utilization rate from 1965 to the present. Here again we observe a phenomenon with which we are familiar by now: the apparent establishment of new norms in the 1970s as compared to the second half of the 1960s. The lowest unemployment rate in the later period is substantially higher than the highest in the earlier, and the highest utilization rate in the 1970s is well below the lowest in the second half of the 1960s. Despite all the pumping with its attendant price inflation, the economy has been limping along at far less than its officially rated capacity. Moreover, except in the area of prices, the responsiveness of the system to more and more vigorous pumping seems to be on the decline.

TABLE 6
Unemployment and Manufacturing Capacity Utilization

	Unemployment as Percent of Civilian Labor Force	*Percent of Manufacturing Capacity Utilized*
1965	4.5	89.0
1966	3.8	91.9
1967	3.8	87.9
1968	3.6	87.7
1969	3.5	86.5
1970	4.9	78.3
1971	5.9	75.0
1972	5.6	78.6
1973	4.9	83.0

Source: *Ibid*, pp. 279, 291.

Such was the situation which existed as the economy entered one of its regular cyclical downswings, this time aggravated and intensified by the so-called energy crisis and a worldwide shortage of food which has greatly increased the demand for U.S. agricultural exports and sent domestic food prices sky high. Meanwhile, President Nixon has "promised" in his State of the Union message that there will be no recession, and a White House official has been quoted (in the February *Morgan Guaranty Survey*) as saying: "The President is very firm about that [avoiding a recession]. If it means busting the budget he will bust the budget rather than keep people out of jobs." Not that busting the budget—and other pumping operations which would doubtless go along with it—would necessarily succeed in preventing a recession, but it undoubtedly would accelerate the already raging process of inflation. What we seem likely to get therefore is both a recession and still more inflation.

Is there any alternative? Yes, of course there is. Let the recession take its natural course and turn into a full-fledged depression. Then let the depression get as bad as necessary to deflate the debt and price structure, which has always been the functional role of panics and depressions in the operation of capitalism. Finally, start all over again in a situation from which the worst distortions and disproportions produced by decades of inflation have been squeezed out.

The trouble of course is that this is roughly what happened after 1929, and the experience was so traumatic for the rulers of capitalism that they vowed never to let it happen again. Fortunately for them, at least so it seemed, John Maynard Keynes came along at about this time with what he claimed to be the solution of the problem. Keynes argued that the capitalist system could be rescued from depression and kept on a more or less stable high-employment plateau by a suitable combination of fiscal and monetary policies (deficit government spending and increasing the money supply, two closely related processes, as we have already seen). This prescription was eagerly accepted not only by most economists but by the ruling classes of the advanced capitalist countries. Putting the Keynesian strategy into practice required that there should be acceptable and suitably large objects of government spending, as well as a flexible money-and-credit system. The first of these conditions was never fulfilled during the 1930s, with the result that even at the top of the cyclical upswing in 1937 more than 14 percent of the labor force was still unemployed. But with the coming of the Second World War, followed almost immediately by the Cold War, all that changed. Huge and rising military budgets became the order of the day, and the money-and-credit system proved fully able to carry its share of the load.

Thus since the Second World War every time a recession looked as though it might get worse and turn into an old-fashioned depression, the reaction of the governing circles was to turn on the deficit-spending and money-and-credit spigots. It was conceded that this would involve a certain amount of inflation—maybe two or three percent a year—but that has always been considered better for capitalism than price stability, not to speak of price deflation. For a long time all seemed to be for the best in the best of all possible capitalist worlds.

What was ignored—and still seems to be recognized only by Marxists on the Left and financial conservatives on the Right—is that this strategy necessarily involves a secular increase in society's debt structure, with a parallel decline in corporate and individual liquidity.* Thus the economy became more and

* On this, see "The Long-Run Decline in Liquidity," *Monthly Review*, September 1970; reprinted in Paul M. Sweezy and Harry Magdoff, *The*

more vulnerable to the kind of shocks which in the old days used to touch off panics; and in order to guard against this recurring threat, the need for still more inflation becomes increasingly acute. Thus the near panic triggered by the Penn Central bankruptcy in 1970 was countered by a massive injection of Federal Reserve credit. Price increases, a bloated credit structure, feverish speculation all had to be tolerated and actually spurred on in order to stave off the dreaded deflation which in times gone by was capitalism's "natural" cure for such ills.

We have already reviewed figures indicating how busy the inflationary pumps have been these past three years, without however bringing the economy as a whole anywhere near a satisfactory level of utilization of its human and material resources. The Keynesian chickens, so freely released from the coop these past three decades, are coming home to roost with a vengeance. The gentle, stimulating, two to three percent inflation which used to be envisaged and welcomed has turned into a raging flood which is wildly out of control and beyond the possibility of measurement by any one of the traditional indexes. A better idea of the reality, including the prospects for the period ahead, is conveyed by the following statement from the "Business Outlook" section of *Business Week* for February 23rd:

> If there was any question that 1974 would be an inflationary year, it was quickly answered by the year's first price figures: wholesale prices rocketed off in January to one of the biggest one-month increases ever.
>
> The Bureau of Labor Statistics' broad wholesale price index rose to 150.4 (1967=100) in the month, bringing it 20.8 percent above last January.
>
> Of course fuel prices were an important contributor to the advance. They alone accounted for 40 percent of the monthly increase.

Dynamics of U.S. Capitalism, Monthly Review Press, 1972, pp. 180-196. We have not thought it worthwhile to publish here up-to-date figures on corporate liquidity because the intervening period is too short to lend much weight to arguments about the shape of long-run trends going back to the Second World War. What can be said by way of summary is that, as typically happens in the downs phase of the cycle, there was a small improvement in corporate liquidity ratios from 1970 to 1971, but that thereafter the downward slide resumed and the latest figures show that in some asset classes liquidity ratios by mid-1973 were back to or below those of 1970 There is no reason to assume that the long-run has been altered.

> But prices are shooting up virtually everywhere. Farm products rose 8.1 percent in the month, and processed food and feeds rose 3.1 percent. . . .
>
> Of the 13 major industrial price categories, only one—lumber and wood products—showed a decline in the month. But that category was still almost 22 percent above a year ago. . . .

All of this, taken together with declining industrial production and rising unemployment, has prompted the First National City Bank to headline one section of its January *Monthly Economic Letter*: "Roaring Worldwide Inflation Confronts Policymakers with a Hard Decision: Accept a Full-blown Recession or Pump Up the Money Supply and Boost Prices Even Further."

Jacob Morris, writing in the September 1973 issue of *Monthly Review,* put the matter succinctly when he compared inflation with a drug which had turned from being tonic to being toxic. He might have added that the patient, worldwide monopoly capitalism, has now become so addicted to this poison that it must go on increasing the dose. The alternative is a drying-out period so horrendous in its implications that it is doubtful the system could survive the ordeal.

The irony is that it may be no better able to survive the poison.

But unlike human beings, social systems do not die of their own accord. They have to be overthrown by human agents who find their ills no longer tolerable. That such agents in the shape of the working people who are the system's main victims will eventually step forward on the stage of history and take in hand the great task of saving not only themselves but all humanity—this need not be doubted, indeed cannot be doubted by anyone who believes that humanity has a future. But how soon it will happen, and what forms the struggle will take, we are still not in a position to foresee.

Banks: Skating on Thin Ice

January 1975

> By means of the banking system the distribution of capital as a special business, a social function, is taken out of the hands of the private capitalists and usurers. But at the same time, banking and credit thus become the most effective means of driving capitalist production beyond its own limits and one of the most effective vehicles of crises and swindle.
>
> —Marx, *Capital,* vol. 3

The specter haunting today's capitalist world is the possible collapse of its financial institutions and an associated world economic crisis. The miasma of fear is hardly surprising in the light of the coincidence in many capitalist countries of seemingly uncontrollable inflation, declining production, and instability in financial markets. The banking and credit community is showing increasing signs of weakness. Thus, in the span of one year the United States witnessed the two largest bank failures in its history (U.S. National Bank in San Diego and Franklin National Bank in New York). In addition, according to a report in the *Wall Street Journal* of December 18, 1974, more than a dozen European banks reported big losses or failed in 1974.

The state of mind of the ruling classes of the leading capitalist countries was well illustrated in an article in *Le Monde* (October 22, 1974), Europe's most prestigious newspaper,

This article originally appeared in the February 1975 issue of *Monthly Review.*

entitled "The Bankers of New York Begin to Feel the Wind of Panic." According to the paper's special correspondent in New York, he was told by a well-known American banker:

> "It is not impossible that the monetary authorities will be led in the near future to make dramatic decisions, such for example as freezing certain long-term deposits in the banks (deposits established against the issuance of CDs, i.e., certificates of deposit for which there is a very active market in the United States). It is not even possible to exclude the possibility of a panic which would drive depositors to withdraw their funds."
>
> These somber prognostications, made during a luncheon attended by some ten people, raised no objections from the other guests, whose analyses in other respects however were quite different from those of our interlocutor, a man with world-wide experience, not confined only to the United States.

Superficial apologists are inclined to gloss over these warning signals by dwelling solely on the special and, by implication, unique errors of the banks that collapsed, thereby ignoring the fact that these so-called errors are merely distorted reflections of more basic difficulties besetting the money markets. The more responsible financial leaders of the capitalist class tend to speak more frankly. For example, Robert V. Roosa, a partner in Brown Brothers Harriman and former Undersecretary of the Treasury, observed last August, according to a *Washington Post* dispatch:

> "There has been a loss of confidence in the [financial] machinery most of us took for granted. There is a fear, a kind of foreboding." It is "not too much," Roosa added, to say that these concerns are similar to the kind that prevailed in the 1930s. (Published in the *Boston Globe,* August 5, 1974)

And the chairman of the Federal Reserve Board, Arthur F. Burns, in a major address to the latest convention of the American Bankers Association (October 21, 1974) also went back to the Great Depression as a point of comparison for today's critical conditions. While he did not specifically identify the decade of the 1930s, he could not have meant anything else by his opening sentence: "This year, for the first time in decades, questions have been raised about the strength of the nation's, and indeed the world's, banking system." Rather than sweep this notion under the rug, as one might expect from a conservative government official charged with the responsibility to sustain the public confidence and faith on which banks rely to stay in business, Burns went on to spell out in considerable detail why such fears are justified, tracing the problems to the fact that the "goals of profitability and growth have been receiving more and more attention [by bank managements]." He did, of course, utter the necessary endorsement of faith in the banks, but made it clear that it does not rest on the liquidity and stability of the banks themselves. Instead, he pointed out that "for the first time since the Great Depression, the availability of liquidity from the central bank has become . . . an essential ingredient in maintaining confidence in the commercial banking system. . . . Faith in our banks . . . now rests unduly on the fact that troubled banks can turn to a governmental lender of last resort." (Full text of Burns's speech in *The American Banker*, October 23, 1974.)

Why is it that matters have been permitted to reach such a state—where banks can't stand on their own feet and must hopefully rely on the government to prevent collapse? Why, indeed, when there are long-established laws and regulatory bodies—notably, the Federal Reserve Board itself—designed to prevent precisely the dangerous developments analyzed coldly and competently by Burns in the aforementioned speech? Surely, the reason can't be ignorance. The relevant data about the operations of the large commercial banks are available to the Federal Reserve Board, and are publicly distributed by the Board itself, from week to week. Moreover, the important changes, showing increasing sources of instability, are not new, but, as we shall show below, have been developing since the early 1960s and accelerating since the mid-1960s.

The answers to these questions are not to be found in ignorance, absence of wisdom, or lack of will power. What has to be understood is that the ruling class and government officials could hardly have prevented the present situation from developing no matter how much they may have wanted to. The overextension of debt and the overreach of the banks was exactly what was needed to protect the capitalist system and its profits; to overcome, at least temporarily, its contradictions; and to support the imperialist expansion and wars of the United States.

Those who now complain and tremble over excesses are the very same people who helped bring them about, or at the least did nothing to forestall them, for fear of bringing down the whole financial network. This should become clearer as we examine some of the key facts.

Before we get into the workings of the banking system in these years of inflation and credit expansion, we should understand that there are two sides to the debt explosion: (1) capitalists borrow as much as possible not only from necessity but, more importantly, as a way to increase their individual profit rates, and (2) banks and other institutions aggressively increase their lending as a means of maximizing their own profits. The first point can easily be seen with a simple arithmetical illustration.

Investment—First Stage	
Let us assume that a capitalist has invested in a manufacturing process	$ 1,000
Profit	
Assume that he makes a gross profit of 20% on this investment	$ 200
Assume further that he pays 50% of profits in taxes	$ –100
He then makes a net profit of 10% on his investment	$ 100
Investment—Second Stage	
The capitalist decides to double his capacity, but, instead of plowing back his profits, he borrows another $1,000 by issuing bonds. The capital in his business then consists of	
Stock investment	$ 1,000
Bonds	$ 1,000
Total capital	$ 2,000
Profit	
Gross profit (20%) on total capital	$ 400
Assume bondholders are paid 6% interest on their $1,000 of bonds	$ –60
The capitalist then has, after interest payments	$ 340
Deduct the 50% he pays in taxes	$ –170
The capitalist now gets a profit rate of 17% on his original $1,000 invested	$ 170

This arithmetic of profits (in our simplified example, a

potential increase in the profit rate from 10 to 17 percent) is what lies behind a good deal of the vast expansion of long-term debt shown in Table 1.

TABLE I
Investment in All U.S. Corporations

Year	*Long-term debt bonds and mortgages*	*Direct investment by owners of the corporation: stocks*	*Long-term debt as a percent of stock investment*
	Billions of dollars		
1940	$ 49	$ 89	55.1%
1950	66	94	70.2
1955	98	113	86.7
1960	154	140	110.0
1965	210	161	130.4
1970	363	201	180.6

Source: *Statistical Abstract of the United States: 1973* (Washington, D.C.: U S. Bureau of the Census, 1973), p. 479.

As can clearly be seen from Table 1, the rapid accumulation of corporate capital since the end of the Great Depression involved both equity investment and debt, but the growth in the use of bonds and mortgages far outpaced that of stocks. Stock investment (equity capital) increased $112 billion (from $89 in 1940 to $201 billion in 1970), while debt capital (bonds and mortgages) grew by $314 billion (from $49 in 1940 to $363 billion in 1970). This shift to much greater use of debt capital has two origins: (1) the drive to increase profit rates, as explained in the foregoing arithmetical example; and (2) the constant pressure to increase the mass of profits, even though, as in Marx's words cited at the outset, this means "driving capitalist production beyond its own limits," and means relying on debt because of the insufficiency of funds capitalists are able to generate internally or through flotation of new stock issues to finance expansion. Note that we are now discussing all corporations (financial and nonfinancial); the impulse to rely on borrowed money for investment capital extends over the entire spectrum of capitalist enterprise.

As much as this long-term debt of corporations has grown, it has nevertheless proven to be insufficient to appease the capitalist appetite for accumulation. And hence corporations, with the collaboration of the banks and other financial institutions, began to depend more and more on short-term borrowing as a means of obtaining capital both for new investment in plant and equipment and for their everyday operations. Salient facts on these changes for all nonfinancial corporations are shown in Table 2.

TABLE 2

Short-term Debt of Nonfinancial Corporations

End of year	*Bank loans*	*Other borrowing(a)*	*Gross National Product originating in nonfinancial corporations*	*Bank loans as percent of GNP*	*Other borrowing as percent of GNP*
	Billions of dollars				
1950	$18.3	$ 1.4	$151.7	12.1%	.9%
1955	25.6	3.0	216.3	11.8	1.4
1960	37.7	6.8	273.1	13.8	2.5
1965	60.7	8.8	377.6	16.1	2.3
1970	102.5	24.3	516.1	19.9	4.7
1974 (first half)	183.6	37.6	727.9	25.2	5.2

a. Includes commercial paper sold by corporations on the open market and loans by finance companies.

Source: Data for borrowing are from *Flow of Funds Accounts 1945-1972* (Board of Governors of the Federal Reserve System, August 1973) for 1960 and previous years; *Federal Reserve Bulletin,* October 1974, for the period after 1960. Data for gross national product originating in nonfinancial corporations are from *The Economic Report of the President* (Washington, D.C.: U.S. Govt. Printing Office, 1974) for the data prior to 1974; and the *Survey of Current Business,* October 1974, for first half of 1974.

Especially noteworthy in the data presented in Table 2 is the marked difference between the years before and after 1960. Bank loans increased in the decade of the 1950s, but pretty much in line with the general expansion of nonfinancial corporate business: bank loans as a percent of nonfinancial corporate GNP were 12.1 in 1950 and 13.8 in 1960—a rise, but not an especially significant one. Other short-term borrowing also grew in this period, but in 1960 it was still small potatoes. Now look at the decisive change that begins with 1960. Between 1960 and 1974 bank loans grew at a much faster rate than nonfinancial business activity, the ratio of the former to the latter almost doubling: from 13.8 percent in 1960 to 25.2 percent in the first half of 1974, while at the same time other forms of short-term borrowing spurted forward.

Still more interesting is the acceleration in the dependence on bank credit. Thus, if we examine the rate of increase of this dependency (as expressed in the column of Table 2 headed "Bank loans as percent of GNP"), we find that reliance on bank credit increases by 17 percent between 1960 and 1965, by 24 percent in the next five-year period, and by 27 percent in only three-and-a-half years from the end of 1970 to the end of June 1974.

While this kind of debt acceleration helps keep the economy going by "driving capitalist production beyond its limits," the dependence on debt produces limits of its own. If we assume for the sake of argument that the sale of bonds and mortgages and the granting of bank loans can keep on increasing endlessly, business borrowers can still absorb this expanding debt only as long as they can make enough profit to meet the rising interest payments. Eventually, if the debt load keeps accelerating, the interest on the debt begins to choke off profits and hence also the incentive, as well as the financial ability, to keep the underlying accumulation process going.

The capitalist answer to this dilemma up to now has been to feed the fires of inflation. As interest burdens increase—the result of larger debt as well as higher interest rates stimulated by the huge demand for money capital—capitalists raise prices to meet these obligations. And as price hikes spread throughout the economy, the need for even more borrowing follows. Thus debt obligations, interest charges, and prices chase each other in the upward spiral of inflation.

Thus far we have examined only one side of the problem: the demand for money by business, assuming in effect that there is no end to the supply of money. To a certain extent, this is a tenable assumption, but only if one also assumes that the government's money-printing presses go mad and end up producing a hyperinflation that destroys the country's currency. Short of such a runaway inflation, we are beginning to see obstacles emerging in the ability of the banks to keep on supplying credit at the accelerated rate of the past. It is true that the banks, in pursuit of ever more profits for themselves, have tried to keep up with the demand for loans. But in doing so they have stretched themselves so thin that their own liquidity is in question, and legitimate fears have been raised about the possible collapse of the financial system.

To understand this aspect of the problem we need to review a few simple fundamentals of how commercial banks operate. The traditional function of such banks has been to act as a depository (safekeeper) of money. Individuals and business firms place their money in these banks in the form of deposits in checking or savings accounts, which the banks should always be able to return on request. The banks in turn accept these deposits because they can make a profit by using the major part of them either to buy bonds or to make loans. Bankers base their operations on the assumption of a certain pattern of withdrawal of deposits by customers, i.e., that only a certain portion will be withdrawn each day. To meet these withdrawals, banks keep a reserve of cash. Since one cannot be too sure that there may not be unexpected surges of deposit withdrawals, an additional part of the deposits is invested in short-term U.S. Treasury bills and notes. The prices of these investments do not fluctuate very much and, more important, they can be sold almost instantaneously in the money market to raise cash, should deposit withdrawals suddenly increase. On top of this, banks invest another part of the deposits in longer-term bonds of the U.S. Treasury, other government bodies, and corporations. On such investments banks make more money than on short-term debt instruments, their disadvantage being that the prices of these bonds fluctuate, which means that the banks can lose money if they are forced to sell when prices are down. Still more profitable for the banks than bonds are loans to businesses and consumers, but these cannot normally be turned into cash until they mature, so they provide little or no protection against a sudden dash by depositors to withdraw funds. Hence, for the sake of safety, banks have traditionally maintained a pattern of investment which consists of retaining a margin of ready cash and then distributing their money-making assets among a variety of notes, bonds, and loans.

Against this background look at Table 3, which shows how banking practices have been changing in recent years and why doubts have been arising about the general viability of the banking system.

The rise in the percent of loans to deposits between 1950 and 1960 is not especially noteworthy. Cash reserves in banks (and in business firms) were still very large, reflecting the cash accumulated during the Second World War. Further, the fact that 56 percent of the deposits of the large commercial banks were loaned out still left the banks in a fairly secure position, with comfortable reserves in cash and short-term securities to meet emergencies. It is the inexorable growth of the percentage of loans to deposits since 1960 that cries out for attention. The heating up of the economy under the stimulus of the Vietnam War and the consequent kindling of the flames of inflation induced an expansion of the bank-lending activity beyond any traditional understanding of the so-called fiduciary responsibility of the banks, a process that endangers the safety of the money left for safekeeping and begins to bump against the ultimate ceiling of how much money banks can lend.

Clearly, the banks cannot lend out all of their deposits; some part must be held in reserve to pay depositors who wish to withdraw their money and to cover losses arising from defaulted loans. While there is no trustworthy guide to the "proper" ratio of loans to deposits, the persistent rise in the ratio, especially since 1970, reveals that even apart from their responsibility as safekeepers of other people's money, the banks are fast approaching the absolute limit (100 percent) of the deposits that could be loaned out. Thus, as shown in Table 3, by the end of 1974 the large commercial banks had committed 82 percent of their deposits to loans; the same pattern is seen in the large New York City banks—at the heart of the country's main money market. To see this in perspective, it should be noted that the highest ratio of loans to deposits in U.S. banks between 1900 and 1970 was 79 percent (and that in only one year, 1921); in 1929 the ratio was 73.1 percent. (Calculated from data in U.S. Bureau of the Census, *Historical Statistics of the United States, Colonial Times to 1957,* Washington, D.C., 1960.)

How the banks were able to reach the extraordinary ratios of the 1970s will be explained below. But for the present it should be noted that a sizable part of the deposits recorded in Table 3 are far from what would be considered "normal" deposits of banks. No less than 40 percent of the deposits of the large New York City banks consists of large certificates of deposit, money borrowed by banks to facilitate the rapid growth of loans beyond otherwise practical limits; and half the increase in these deposits between 1965 and 1974 was generated by the sale of these specially issued short-term certificates of deposit. But more on this later.

This is not yet the whole story. In their search for profits and since they are bumping against limits to their outright lending power, the banks have introduced and are expanding a new technique of lending, called "standby letters of credit." (See *Business Week,* February 16, 1974, p. 120.) For a fee, they guarantee the IOUs issued and sold on the commercial paper market by big corporations. In other words, the banks commit themselves to paying the borrowed money if the corporations default. Since it is the financially weaker corporations that need such bank guarantees in order to sell their IOUs, this type of "indirect loan" is itself of the shakier variety. These letters of credit are not reported on the balance sheets of the banks and are therefore not included in the loan figures shown in Table 3. If they were included, the 1974 percentages of loans to deposits would be even larger than those shown.

Why this mad rush by the banks to expand loans? There are two basic reasons: the lust for profit and the pressure of competition. Banks operate according to the laws of capitalism expounded by Marx. Their dominant motive is the continuous search for ways to expand profits: by accumulating capital and by increasing their rate of profit. They search in every nook and cranny of the economy, using salesmen, newspaper and television advertising, testing new devices—all geared to opening up new opportunities both for lending large amounts to

TABLE 3

Loans and Deposits: Commercial Banks

End of year	*Loans*	*Deposits*	*Loans as percent of deposits*
	Billions of dollars		
	LARGE COMMERCIAL BANKS(a)		
1950	$ 31.6	$ 87.7	36.0%
1955	48.4	105.3	46.0
1960	71.6	127.2	56.3
1965	120.3	181.8	66.2
1970	188.8	266.8	70.8
1974	319.3	389.4	82.0
	LARGE NEW YORK CITY BANKS		
1950	$ 9.9	$25.1	39.4%
1955	14.2	27.9	50.9
1960	18.6	31.0	60.0
1965	31.8	45.7	69.6
1970	45.5	63.2	72.0
1974	78.9	93.5	84.4

a. Banks that had total deposits of $100 million or more on Dec. 31, 1965.

Source: Data prior to 1974 are from various issues of the *Federal Reserve Bulletin*. Data for 1974 are from *Federal Reserve Statistical Release H.4.3* for the last week in 1974.

business firms, real estate operators, stock market speculators, finance companies, and also for extending small loans (at even higher rates of interest) to the garden-variety of citizen. This incessant drive for business and profits goes on even as the banks' lending potential (as shown in Table 3) narrows; in this fashion, they are being true to their nature as capitalist entrepreneurs.

The second stimulus for the ballooning of loans is the competition among the banks themselves. Turning down the request for a loan to an established customer always carries with it the threat that the borrower will shift his entire banking business to a competitor. If the customer is a big corporation, there is every reason to expect that another bank will stretch itself to latch on to a new source of business, even if the loan in question does not measure up to "sound" banking practice.

Both of these pressures—the drive for profits and the need to protect one's already existing market—lead to a larger and larger share of relatively unsafe loans in the banks' portfolios. It should be noted that the very ease with which the larger corporations can get loans facilitates their carrying on their own business affairs beyond safe limits, as clearly seen in the steady decline in the ratio of liquid reserves relative to what the corporations owe. (See "The Long-Run Decline in Corporate Liquidity," in *Monthly Review,* September 1970.) And the harder it becomes for the corporations to repay their bank loans (because of declining liquidity), the more the banks are obliged to grant further loans to prevent borrowers from going bust and thus defaulting on the backlog of loans. As willing or unwilling collaborators in the process by which the large corporations operate closer and closer to the edge of the precipice, the banks are themselves drawn nearer to the same edge, for they can manage to lend at such a furious rate only by impairing their own liquidity. What has been happening on this score is shown in Table 4.

TABLE 4

Liquidity of Large Commercial Banks

End of year	*Cash Reserves(a)*	*U.S. Treasury Bonds(b)*	*Short-term U.S. Treasury Notes(c)*	*Cash + All Treasuries as a percent of total deposits(d)*	*Cash + Short-term Treasuries as a percent of total deposits(d)*
	Billions of dollars				
1950	$13.7	$33.7	n.a.	54.0%	n.a.
1955	14.9	30.1	n.a.	42.7	n.a.
1960	14.0	30.2	$ 8.2	34.7	17.5%
1965	16.3	24.3	8.6	22.3	13.7
1970	20.2	28.1	10.3	18.3	11.4
1974	29.5	23.4	7.9	13.6	9.6

n.a.: Not available.

a. Cash in vault plus reserves with Federal Reserve banks, as required by the Federal Reserve Board.

b. Bonds here include bills, certificates, notes, as well as bonds.

c. All treasury securities that mature in less than one year.

d. The data on deposits used as the denominator are those given in Table 3.

Source: Same as Table 3.

The last two columns of Table 4 are measures of the liquid position of the banks. In other words, they show what percentage of deposits can be got hold of quickly by bank managements to pay back depositors' money in case of an upsurge of withdrawals. The decline in liquidity shown in the penultimate column of this table (the persistent decline from 54 percent in 1950 to under 14 percent in 1974) should come as no surprise after one has examined Table 3, for this decline has been a necessary complement to the increasing percentage of loans to deposits. (This inverse relation is not precisely complementary because of the growth of bank borrowing, as will be explained presently.) Yet even this meager liquidity ratio exaggerates the reserve position of the large commercial banks. First, in order for a bank to qualify as a depository for U.S. Treasury funds, it must keep a specified reserve of U.S. treasuries to back up the government's deposits. Hence, not all of the treasuries included in this liquidity ratio would be available to meet sudden large drains on deposits. Second, the data shown in the third column represent what the banks originally paid for the bonds. (This is standard accounting practice for bank assets.) The market prices of bonds, however, go up and down: as interest rates rise the prices of bonds go down, and vice versa. For example, if a bank wanted to sell a twenty-year, 3-percent Treasury bond which had been bought for $1,000 (and so recorded on the bank's books), all that could be realized on that bond in the market at the end of 1974 would have been about $550. Furthermore, if several big banks began to unload their bond holdings quickly, the market price would drop even further.

It follows that the data in the penultimate column of Table 4 overstate the degree of liquidity, sharp as the drop shown has been. A more realistic picture is given in the last column of the table, where only the short-term treasuries (those with a maturity of less than one year) are counted. And here we see the same pattern: a persistent decline in liquidity, dropping by almost half from 17.5 percent in 1960 to 9.6 percent in 1974. There is an interesting feature here that is worth noting. If you look at the first column, you can see that cash reserves have been rising since 1960, not as much as the growth in deposits but a significant increase nevertheless. The reason that the banks did this was because they were forced to in order to live up to the requirements of the Federal Reserve Board. But for the next most liquid asset—short-term treasuries—there is no such pressure from the Board. What the banks do with respect to short-term treasuries is their own business. So here the investment by the large commercial banks was actually *reduced* somewhat between 1960 and 1974 while their liabilities in the form of deposits were more than tripling during the same period.*

Liquidity ratios are not the only way of looking at the safety problem. Traditional theory of good banking practice points out that while loans are a source of risk, banks protect themselves by maintaining special reserves in reasonable anticipation of a certain percentage of defaults, and in the final analysis rely on the bank's equity capital (bank stockholders' original investment plus accumulated profits) to make good on unexpected loan losses (thus preventing loss of deposits). But here too the ratio of equity capital to outstanding loans has been steadily dropping, most noticeably since 1960, as pointed out by Arthur Burns in the speech quoted above:

> . . . this enormous upsurge in banking assets [in other words, increase in loans] has far outstripped the growth of bank capital. At the end of 1960, equity capital plus loan and valuation reserves amounted to almost 9 percent of total bank assets. By the end of 1973, this equity capital ratio had fallen to about 6½ percent. Furthermore, the equity capital banks had been leveraged in some cases at the holding company level, as parent holding companies have increased their equity investments in subsidiary

* One of the common illusions concerning this subject is the belief that even if bank liquidity is inadequate the Federal Deposit Insurance Corporation (FDIC) is at hand to protect the savings of depositors. The truth is that the FDIC is only an insurance company and can therefore rescue depositors only to the extent that it has enough assets to cover bank losses. Thus, as an insurance agency the FDIC was designed to deal with occasional breakdowns of one or more banks, and not with a major financial catastrophe. The dimensions of the problem can be seen from the following facts. According to the last annual report of the FDIC, the deposits covered by FDIC insurance amounted to $465.6 billion at the end of 1973. Against this the FDIC had $8.6 billion: $5.6 billion of assets, plus the right to borrow, according to existing law, $3 billion from the U.S. Treasury.

banks by using funds raised in the debt markets. Thus, the capital cushion that plays a large role in maintaining confidence in banks has become thinner, particularly in some of our largest banking organizations.

For a better understanding of Burns's argument we should know something about bank holding companies. A "loophole" in the amendments to the 1956 Bank Holding Company Act has been used by most of the big banks to expand their activities into a diverse range of nontraditional financial operations. What happens is that a holding company is set up which owns a bank and at the same time may own, for example, mortgage, finance, and factoring businesses. A number of these bank holding companies have gone to the money market to borrow funds in order to carry on this variety of operations, and in the process have used some of the borrowed money to increase their equity investment in their own banks. This is what Burns is referring to: even that small ratio of equity capital to assets is overstated, since some of the equity is really only debt owed by the parent company.

And now we come to where the dog is buried. How do banks manage in practice to keep on extending loans to reach such percentages as shown in Table 3? Normally, banks get resources to meet the demand for loans by increasing their capital, attracting additional deposits, or selling off investments in bonds. As we have just seen, the increase in equity capital was insufficient to support the explosion in loans. Nor have deposits increased sufficiently. Finally, the banks did not want to take the losses that would result from selling off all or a major part of their bond holdings, assuming that they could do so without destroying the market for bonds. So beginning in the 1960s the banks themselves have become major borrowers in order to enable them to indulge in their furious rush to lend. In the process they have created a complex network of borrowing and lending throughout the business world which not only further stimulated the inflationary process, but also resulted in a kind of delicately balanced debt structure that is constantly in danger of breaking down. Now let us look at the facts as shown in Tables 5 and 6. (See pp. 48-49.)

Before discussing the significance of the facts presented

TABLE 5
Short-Term Borrowing by Large Commercial Banks

	Borrowed money (billions of dollars)					
End of year	*From Federal Reserve Banks and others*	*Federal funds purchased*(a)	*Large negotiable certificates of deposit*(b)	*Eurodollars*(c)	*Total*	*Short-term borrowing as a percent of total loans outstanding*(d)
1950	$0.7	—	—	—	$ 0.7	2.2%
1960	1.8	$ 1.4	—	—	3.2	4.5
1965	6.2	2.6	$16.1	—	24.9	20.7
1970	1.5	18.8	26.1	$7.7	54.1	28.7
1974	4.8	54.0	92.2	4.0	155.0	48.5

a. The data for 1960 and 1965 are from a special series designed by the Federal Reserve Board, based on the 46 most active commercial banks in the federal funds market. The data for these years are not comparable with those for later years, but are given here to indicate the trend. The data for 1970 and 1974 include, in addition to federal funds purchased, securities sold under agreements to repurchase identical or similar securities, and sales of participations in pools of securities.

b. These are short-term certificates of deposit issued in minimum amounts of $100,000.

c. These data are the reported "Gross Liabilities of Banks to Their Foreign Branches." According to the Federal Reserve Bank of New York, *Glossary: Weekly Federal Reserve Statements,* this item is often used as a proxy for Eurodollar borrowings, though these data include some other types of transactions between domestic banks and their foreign branches.

d. The data on loans used as the denominator are those given in Table 3.

Source: Same as Table 3.

in these tables, let us first explain what some of the headings mean. The first item, money borrowed "From Federal Reserve Banks and others," is a catchall, which includes among other things a usually relatively small amount of money that the Federal Reserve Banks lend for a short period to help banks maintain their required reserves, and money borrowed by banks on their promissory notes and other collateral.*

* A description of these various devices, including loan participation certificates, bank-related commercial paper, as well as other items covered in Tables 5 and 6, can be found in Robert E. Knight, "An Alternative Approach to Liquidity, Parts I-IV" in the *Monthly Review* of the Federal Reserve Bank of Kansas City, December 1969 and February, April, May 1970. A shorter version of these questions can be found in Donald M.

TABLE 6

Short-Term Borrowing by Large New York City Commercial Banks

	Borrowed money (billions of dollars)					
End of year	*From Federal Reserve Banks and others*	*Federal funds purchased(a)*	*Large negotiable certificates of deposit(b)*	*Eurodollars(c)*	*Total*	*Short-term borrowing as a percent of total loans outstanding(d)*
1950	$0.4	—	—	—	$ 0.4	4.0%
1960	1.0	$ 0.8	—	—	1.8	9.7
1965	2.5	1.4	$ 6.9	—	10.8	34.0
1970	0.2	5.5	7.9	$5.2	18.8	41.3
1974	1.7	13.6	31.7	2.8	49.8	63.1

a. Same as in Table 5, except that the earlier data are based on a series for eight New York City banks.

b. Same as in Table 5.

c. Same as Table 5, except that the figure for 1974 is estimated, based on past ratios of Eurodollar borrowing by New York City banks to all commercial banks.

d. Same as in Table 5.

Source: Same as Table 3.

The series on "Federal funds purchased" represents, in large measure, borrowings for one business day of excess reserves from other banks willing to lend their funds. There are other borrowing devices included in this category, which as in the case of the federal funds were originally designed to cope with temporary adjustment problems of the banks. But these devices became transformed during the 1960s to meet an entirely different purpose: a tool by the biggest banks to mobilize the maximum of money resources, through going extensively into debt, in order to accelerate the pace of lending.

Still another method of borrowing developed by the big banks in the 1960s was the issuance on a large scale of negoti-

De Pamphilis, "The Short-term Commercial Bank Adjustment Process and Federal Reserve Regulation," in the *New England Economic Review* of the Federal Reserve Bank of Boston, May/June 1974. This is a summary of a more detailed treatment in one section of Federal Reserve Bank of Boston Research Report No. 55 by the same author, *A Microeconomic Econometric Analysis of the Short-term Commercial Bank Adjustment Process.*

able certificates of deposit (CDs) in minimum amounts of $100,000. These too are short-term debts of the banks. Funds raised in this fashion are used to create new loans by the banks which, in addition to being usually of longer duration than the life of the CDs, do not necessarily mature at the same time. This puts the banks under constant pressure to refinance the CDs when they become due, hopefully by issuing still more CDs.

Finally, there is the resort to Eurodollar borrowing. This in effect means the borrowing by U.S. banks from their branches abroad, and is based on the dollar deposits in these foreign branches. This method began to be used in 1966, but became especially important during the credit crunch of 1969. As can be seen from the data for this item shown in the accompanying tables, this method is used intermittently.

There are various technical aspects to these data which need not be gone into here. The important thing is to understand the speculative nature of the enormous debt expansion by the banks—both as borrowers and lenders. On the one hand, the banks are gambling that businesses will be able to repay their loans despite (1) declining corporate liquidity, and (2) the fact that many firms are borrowing to pay for investment in plant and equipment that will take longer to produce the income needed than is required by the loan repayment schedules. On the other hand, the banks are speculating on being able to support this large and growing lending by having recourse to the mercurial money markets. How rapidly this short-term borrowing has grown and how dependent banks have become on this type of debt to expand their loan load is shown in Tables 5 and 6. From Table 5 we learn that the reliance on short-term borrowing by the large commercial banks reached a point by the end of 1974 such that it represented almost 50 percent of outstanding loans. Even more striking is the case of the large New York City commercial banks, where, as can be seen in Table 6, 63 percent of their outstanding loans is accounted for by short-term borrowing.

It is also important to understand the degree of uncertainty involved in these various forms of borrowing by the banks. They are almost all interest-sensitive, which means that the quantity of such borrowing can fluctuate very widely over relatively short periods, depending on the interest differentials for various types of borrowing. Arthur Burns in the previously quoted speech refers to the "volatile character" of these borrowings. And it is on these foundations that the equally volatile structure of loans, which keep the economy going, is based.

In short, the commercial banking structure, and the entire business world that relies on this structure, is skating on thin ice that is getting progressively thinner.

Why haven't the powers-that-be done something about this? As noted above, there is good reason to believe that all this has been well known for some time by the government agencies set up to prevent such menacing developments. From time to time, these agencies, and in particular the Federal Reserve Board, have taken steps to moderate one or more abuses, only to find that the financial community either found a loophole in the regulations or discovered another avenue to stretch out the debt load. Basically, the regulatory agencies were helpless, despite all their bold stances, because they too were committed to the same ends as the ruling financial and other business circles: to increase profits and to expand business opportunities, with all that these ends entail, including imperialist expansion and the Vietnam War. Rowing in the same boat as the business community, the regulators had to close their eyes to the dangers, trusting in lucky stars. Once the excesses began to reach a critical point it was too late to retreat, for too much disturbance of the intricate and complexly interrelated debt structure could all too easily break the thin ice.

The transformations described here also illuminate how fanciful are the myths of economists, Keynesians and non-Keynesians alike, who insist that they can produce a smoothly running capitalist economy by manipulation of such matters as fiscal policy, interest rates, and the money supply. The point is that all such devices do not get to the heart of what makes the capitalist economy go.* At best, they cover up for a while

* In addition, hands of the policy-makers are usually tied. It is impossible to devise consistent policies that can at one and the same time handle the conflicting pressures on a capitalist economy: for example, the need to finance the military budget; to keep the money markets in shape to absorb the debts of federal, state, and local governments; to support the

the contradictions of the capitalist system—contradictions that cause eruptions at one time or another—with the credit and banking arrangements being, as Marx long ago explained, at the center of capitalism's vulnerability to crisis.

The advanced thinkers of the ruling class are well aware of the inadequacy of the traditional nostrums as well as of the potential threat of a United States and world-wide depression. They are therefore searching for new and more reliable ways to keep the ship from sinking. It is possible to discern from the business press two important approaches emerging. One is to get the government's finances more actively engaged in salvaging business and banking firms that begin to flounder. This, however, has certain limits, for it entails widening the money and credit stream, and thus reinforcing the inflationary trend. (Over $1 billion, and by some estimates close to $2 billion, was lent by the Federal Reserve to Franklin National, merely the twentieth largest commercial bank at one time, to keep the institution's head above water until some sort of reorganization could be effected, and to sustain public faith in the banking system, thus avoiding a possible flood of withdrawals from other banks. Imagine what would be required if one of the real giants began to gasp!)

The second, and more basic, line of thought is to create a firmer financial foundation for business, so that corporations can rely more on equity capital and less on debt. For this, a greater rate of profit would be needed by business. But that alone would not be enough. The government would have to step in more actively: first, to mobilize federal finances to fatten the equity position of industrial and financial firms; and second, to rationalize monopoly capital by weeding out the weaker firms. Within the limits of capitalism, measures of this sort can have only one meaning: to cut into the living standards (wages and welfare) of the working class, the old-age retirees, the petty bourgeoisie, and smaller businessmen. This is the only way that profit rates can be beefed up and finances procured to

dollar abroad; to improve the balance of payments by attracting foreign funds and stimulating exports; to try to keep inflation from getting completely out of hand; to see that the banks have enough money to rescue tottering corporations; to keep the economy expanding at a rate sufficient to provide jobs for the labor force, etc., etc.

strengthen the equity capital position of the bigger corporations.

Here lies the challenge to the working class and whatever allies may be available to it. Above all, it is necessary to destroy prevailing illusions about the possibility of regulating capitalism in such a way as to produce prosperity for all classes. The ruling class will soon be sharply drawing the class issues with the hope of stabilizing their own affairs. Only by facing up militantly to the fundamental class nature of the impending struggle, which means challenging capitalism as such, does the working class have a chance to protect its true interests.

The Economic Crisis in Historical Perspective—Part I

February 1975

To understand the nature and possible consequences of the present economic crisis, we have to try to put it into proper historical perspective. And in order to do this, we must keep firmly in mind that the real history of capitalism results from the interplay of the inner logic of the system and the changing environment within which it operates. For our present purposes, the crucially important laws of motion inherent in the set of social relations which constitute the capitalist mode of production can be briefly summarized as follows:

(1) Competition of capitals generates concentration and centralization, hence the inevitable replacement of competitive by monopoly capitalism.

(2) The accumulation process is inherently unstable and never tends to take the form of a moving equilibrium (a fantasy of bourgeois economics textbooks). Two forms of motion, attributable to related but distinguishable structural features of the system, characterize the accumulation process: (a) the more or less regular ups and downs of the business cycle (in recent times the length of the cycle, from peak to peak or trough to trough, has tended to be around four years); and (b) a long-range and persistent tendency to stagnation mani-

This article originally appeared in the March 1975 issue of *Monthly Review*.

fested in high rates of unemployment and much idle productive capacity.

(3) The process of monopolization has relatively little effect on the business cycle, but it exacerbates the tendency to stagnation.

It follows from these laws that the *normal* state of the system in its monopoly stage is one of cyclical ups and downs in a context of continuing stagnation. If during any period of time this is not the *actual* state of the system, this fact requires to be explained by historical forces which operate on the system but are not presupposed as being essential to its existence.

In fact, of course, there have been fairly long periods during which the accumulation process has proceeded in a vigorous fashion with (apart from cyclical downswings) the demand for labor power expanding rapidly and productive capacity being utilized at or close to full capacity.* If we examine these periods closely, we find that some combination of the following factors is responsible for the prolonged buoyancy of the accumulation process:

(1) A major innovation involving new technology, new products, and far-reaching changes in the pattern of economic activity. Such were the steam engine in the eighteenth and early nineteenth centuries, the railroad in the second half of the nineteenth century, and the automobile in the twentieth century.

(2) Imperialist expansion and colonial wars.

(3) Wars among the imperialist powers.

(4) Reconstruction after major wars and preparation for new wars.

All of these factors have at one time or another played a

* Over the whole history of capitalism the timing of these periods has varied considerably from country to country, this being one aspect of what Lenin called the law of uneven development. In this essay, unless otherwise indicated, we shall be referring to the United States. At the same time it is important to note that in the last half century there has been a strong trend to greater synchronization among the main capitalist centers. The Great Depression affected the whole capitalist world, as did the secular boom of the 1950s and 1960s. And of course the present crisis has hit all but a handful of oil-rich countries.

crucial role in shaping the course of the accumulation process, in the United States as well as in other parts of the capitalist world. In this country, the railroad directly absorbed about as much capital as all manufacturing and extractive industries combined from the 1850s on, and of course it was indirectly responsible for capital's penetrating the interior of the continent and providing employment for a large part of the great waves of immigrant workers which characterized that period. It can be shown that this "railroad era" came to a rather abrupt end with the (cyclical) panic and depression of 1907, and that nothing came along to take its place until the First World War. Not surprisingly, therefore, the years 1908-1915 were a period of deepening stagnation, with unemployment averaging 6.6 percent of the labor force (more than double the average for the preceding eight-year period), reaching 9.7 percent in 1915.*

What saved the United States from entering a "Great Depression" at that time was the First World War, and what sustained the economy during the 1920s was the first great wave of automobilization, a term which should be interpreted to include not only the development of the automobile industry itself but also many related industries and activities (oil, glass, steel, rubber, highway construction, suburban growth, etc.). The years 1916-1929 were therefore a period of relatively strong expansion and reduced unemployment (average = 4.5 percent), hailed by exuberant economists of the day as a "New Era" which would, in the words of President Herbert Hoover, put a chicken in every pot and a car in every garage.

But the euphoria was short-lived. Nineteen twenty-nine saw the beginning of a regular cyclical downturn; and this time, as had been the case after 1907 only more so, there were no underlying factors of strength to produce a rapid or buoyant recovery. The system's natural tendency to stagnation took over: that monopoly capitalism has no strong internal recuperative power was now demonstrated with brutal clarity.

Politically, the reaction in the United States to the Great

---

* Details in Paul A. Baran and Paul M. Sweezy, *Monopoly Capital* (New York: Monthly Review Press, 1968), pp. 219-234.

Depression was the New Deal, a loosely coordinated set of liberal reformist policies. The New Deal attempted to institute countermeasures, but, apart from alleviating the suffering of the depression's hardest-hit victims, these measures had little effect. The normal business-cycle upswing of the 1930s, which lasted from 1933 to 1937, naturally brought the unemployment rate down, but only from 24.9 percent in 1933 to 14.3 percent, after which it shot up again to 19 percent in the sharp recession of 1938. The key to an understanding of the 1930s—which for a time bourgeois economists like Alvin Hansen and his followers seemed to have grasped, but which even they forgot after the Second World War—was and is that stagnation is the normal and natural condition of monopoly capitalism. During that decade there were no outside stimulating forces of the kind that have always been essential to set capitalism on a sustained upward course.

That is, there were no such forces until the Second World War came along at the very end of the decade. This inaugurated a new period which (for the United States) lasted an extraordinarily long time by previous capitalist standards—a period of some 30 years of expansion, interrupted only by more or less regularly recurring mild recessions.* The driving forces this time were world war, preparation for new wars and waging of large-scale regional wars (Korea and Vietnam), and the second great wave of automobilization.** The reader should be reminded again that automobilization means not only building factories and cars but also highways (now superhighways and freeways) and suburbs, only in recent times the suburbs have been more like extensions of the cities, giving rise to the relatively new

* It is true that the recessions were mild, but the one that commenced in 1958 showed ominous signs of degenerating into stagnation. What came to the rescue was a big increase in war preparations under the Kennedy administration, followed by the Vietnam War itself.

** In the case of the other advanced capitalist countries it was really the first wave of automobilization. And it is worth noting that for the two largest of them, Germany and Japan, recovery from the destruction and prostration of defeat in the Second World War was sparked by orders for armaments and other industrial products stemming, directly and indirectly, from the Korean War.

phenomena of urban sprawl and inner-city decay. There were also many new inventions and technologies, mostly war-related, which played a part in this period, but which by themselves could hardly have been sufficient to prevent the system from sinking into a new phase of stagnation.

All movements of the capitalist economy are accompanied, partly caused, and invariably complicated by their financial aspects, which indeed constitute an absolutely central part of the whole capitalist process. This has been especially, or perhaps it would be better to say spectacularly, true of the long upswing of the 1940s, 1950s, and 1960s.

As a result of shortages, price controls, rationing, and the methods adopted to finance the Second World War, the U.S. economy emerged from that conflict in an unprecedentedly liquid condition. Consumers had pretty well paid off their debts and had savings as well as fresh borrowing power. And the same held true for most businesses, especially the largest ones. For nonfinancial corporations with assets of over $100 million, the average liquidity ratio (cash and government securities divided by short-term debts) was well over 100 percent, while interest charges plus debt repayments absorbed no more than 6 percent of consumer incomes.* The stage was set for the financing of the upswing about to take place through an easy and rapid increase of debt, private and public. This always happens to some extent in upswings: what especially characterizes the one we are now discussing is its length and extent on the one hand, and the proliferation of lending institutions (nurtured hot-house fashion by a multiplicity of government policies and institutions) on the other.

By the end of the 1960s, with the United States being forced by Vietnamese resistance and rising anti-war feeling at home to reduce its military commitment in Southeast Asia, the underlying expansionary forces were clearly weakening, and the long upswing was showing signs of coming to its natural end in a period of stagnation similar to that of the 1930s. What kept things going for a while longer was a truly monumental

---

* For further details, see "The Long-Run Decline in Liquidity," *Monthly Review*, September 1970.

and frantic expansion of debt-financed private and public spending. Given the pervasiveness of monopoly in the U.S. economy—much deeper and more widespread than in the 1920s and 1930s—this burst of debt-financed spending produced a growing inflation of prices which was now superimposed on the incipient downswing of the system as a whole. (For a fuller analysis, see "Keynesian Chickens Come Home to Roost," pp. 21-32 above.)

From that point on we have had to endure at one and the same time two of capitalism's endemic maladies: burgeoning debt and inflation on the one hand, deepening stagnation (as evidence, e.g., by the steadily rising rate of unemployment) on the other. This condition has now been christened by the economic pundits who did not foresee it and can offer no sensible explanation for it. The name is as ugly as the phenomenon itself: stagflation, i.e., stagnation plus inflation, a combination which prior to the maturing of monopoly capitalism would have been considered as impossible as dry water.

To dramatize the situation, let us quote a lengthy passage from *Business Week*, usually a staid and unsensational magazine addressed to business executives. This is from a special supplement to the issue of October 12 entitled "The Debt Economy":

> The U.S. economy stands atop a mountain of debt $2.5 trillion high—a mountain built of all the cars and houses, all the factories and machines that have made this the biggest, richest economy in the history of the world. . . . The U.S. is the Debt Economy without peer. It has the biggest lenders, the biggest borrowers, the most sophisticated financial system. The numbers are so vast that they simply numb the mind: $1-trillion in corporate debt, $600-billion in mortgage debt, $500-billion in U.S. government debt, $200-billion in state and local government debt, $200-billion in consumer debt. To fuel nearly three decades of postwar economic boom at home and export it abroad, this nation has borrowed an average of $200-million a day, each and every day, since the close of World War II. . . .
>
> And there are signs of tension everywhere: corporate debt-equity ratios way out of line, consumer installment-debt repayment taking a record share of disposable income, the huge real-estate market in desperate trouble despite all the federal govern-

ment has done to save it. Never has the Debt Economy seemed more vulnerable, with a distressing number of borrowers and lenders in precarious shape.

Two of the subheads further on in this article read: "No Right Answer" and "A Choice of Disasters." By "A Choice of Disasters," the editors of *Business Week* mean that either the bubble will burst, as it has innumerable times in capitalist history, most recently in the 1930s; or the government will ease its monetary and credit policies and in this way further feed the inflation. What should perhaps be added is that the two "disasters" are not necessarily mutually exclusive.

The big banks and corporations are betting that this time it will not come to a 1930s-type crash because the government will not allow it. Here is what the First National City Bank said in its September *Monthly Economic Letter* (the article is entitled "The Great Depression: History Never Really Repeats Itself"):

> There is—or should be—little doubt that central banks today will assist any major bank whose liquidity has been impaired by general economic conditions. The Fed's passivity in 1930-1933 when faced with widespread bank failures belongs to a different time with a different view of a central bank's role.
>
> And now, in the United States, the Federal Deposit Insurance Corporation stands guard against a re-run of the 1930s. By guaranteeing deposits up to $20,000, it virtually underwrites them as federal obligations. This destroys most of the seeds of public panic.

What New York's largest bank is saying here is that the Federal Reserve will take care of the big boys and the FDIC of the little fellows.*

---

* It should be noted that First National City speaks of assistance to "major" banks. What is likely to happen to those which do not make it to the top rank was illustrated in January when the U.S. Comptroller of the Currency, one of the chief bank regulatory agencies, virtually forced the ailing Security National Bank to sell out to the huge Chemical Bank at a noncompetitive price, thus presenting Chemical at one stroke with scores of prized branch locations on Long Island.

With regard to the FDIC, we pointed out in "Banks: Skating on Thin Ice" (pp. 33-53 above) that as presently set up this is an insurance company with assets grossly inadequate to cope with a *general* col-

This may well be true; in fact we think it probably is. In the Great Depression banks failed in large numbers for some three years before FDR, on coming to office in March 1933, declared a bank holiday. This time it would probably happen immediately the threat became imminent. But this should not give rise in anyone to a false sense of optimism. Forestalling the banking panic of 1930-1933—even if it had been done, as some proposed at the time, by nationalizing the whole banking system—would not have prevented the Great Depression. Nor would it today. The real question is what will happen even if there is no collapse of the banking system, however it may be prevented. Latest official figures put the unemployment rate nationwide at 8.2 percent, the highest recorded since 1941 (9.9 percent); and the Ford administration, abandoning Washington's usual Pollyannish style (for what obscure political reasons we do not pretend to know), has candidly admitted that the rate will remain high by postwar standards for the rest of the decade.* This means in effect that it has now been officially proclaimed that the U.S. economy has entered a new and prolonged period of stagnation.

What does this imply politically? What ruling-class and working-class reactions are likely to develop? What kind of government policies are being talked about, and which stand a chance of being put into practice? These and related questions are discussed in the following chapter.

---

lapse of the banking system. The people at First National • City are obviously assuming that if such a contingency should arise, the government itself would step in and assume responsibility for all insured deposits.

* Whether the projections contained in the President's Economic Report to the Congress, high as they are, don't still reflect an "optimistic" bias is another question. We plan to devote a special study to the whole question of unemployment in an early issue.

The Economic Crisis in Historical Perspective—Part II

March 1975

In the last chapter we argued that U.S. capitalism has once again, as in the 1930s, entered a period of persistent and prolonged stagnation. At the same time we expressed agreement with those who, while recognizing that many big banks and corporations are in very shaky condition, doubt that this time it will come to a 1933-type panic. The expectation of prompt government intervention—through some combination of debt moratoriums and emergency bail-outs—seems well founded. As *Business Week* wrote in its issue of January 27th under the heading, "When Companies Get Too Big to Fail": "The huge U.S. corporations have become such important centers of jobs and incomes that it [the government] dare not let one of them shut down or go out of business. It is compelled, therefore, to shape national policy in terms of protecting the great corporations instead of letting the economy make deflationary adjustments."

If we accept this premise, the question which we ought to try to answer is not *whether* the government will intervene to prevent a panic but what will happen *after* it is forced to intervene. What policies are being discussed in ruling-class

This article originally appeared in the April 1975 issue of *Monthly Review*.

circles? How realistic are they? What are their implications for other sectors of society, and particularly the working class? It is to questions such as these that we now turn our attention.

There is a strong tendency among capitalists and their spokesmen to see all of their troubles as stemming from an insufficiency of surplus value. Profit (one of the components of surplus value) provides the incentive to invest, and the totality of surplus value constitutes the pool from which the capital for additional investment is drawn. Since capitalist prosperity is dependent on a high rate of investment, it seems to follow that what is needed to get the system out of a slump is above all an increase in the amount of surplus value flowing into the pockets of capitalists and other recipients of income derived from surplus value. This will provide, so the argument runs, both the incentive and the wherewithal to increase the rate of investment. The policy implications of this diagnosis are of course obvious: squeeze workers and consumers generally in favor of the corporations and the wealthy. A fairly typical example of this kind of reasoning is contained in *Business Week*'s special supplement on "The Debt Economy" in its issue of last October 12th:

> It is inevitable that the U.S. economy will grow more slowly than it has [an implicit recognition of the new period of stagnation]. . . . Some people will obviously have to do with less. . . . Indeed, cities and states, the home mortgage market, small business, and the consumer, will all get less than they want because the basic health of the U.S. is based on the basic health of its corporations and banks: the biggest borrowers and the biggest lenders. . . .
>
> Put simplistically, as long as corporations stay healthy, they can pay taxes and provide people with jobs. . . . But when corporations fall sick, people lose jobs and stop buying. Nobody pays taxes, governments and local authorities are not financed, and everyone—corporations, consumers, federal and local administrations alike—goes broke or gets embedded more deeply in the debt spiral. . . .
>
> Yet it will be a hard pill for many Americans to swallow—the idea of doing with less so that big business can have more. It will be particularly hard to swallow because it is quite obvious that if big business and big banks are the most visible victims of

what ails the Debt Economy, they are also in large measure the cause of it. . . .

Nothing that this nation, or any other nation, has done in modern history compares in difficulty with the selling job that must now be done to make people accept the new reality. And there are grave doubts whether the job can be done at all. Historian Arnold Toynbee, filled with years and compassion, laments that democracy will be unable to cope with approaching economic problems—and that totalitarianism will take its place.

This is remarkably reminiscent of the remedy prescribed for the German people by its ruling class in 1933. A brutal fascist regime was imposed on the country; all opposition groups, especially those of the working class, were smashed; wages were frozen; and wealth was redistributed in favor of the corporations and the rich. But there was one more essential ingredient of the Nazi success in pulling Germany out of the depression of the 1930s, and that was the enormous expenditures on war preparations which increased employment and stimulated investment both directly and indirectly.

Our analysis of the present situation, put forth in this space last month, leads to the conclusion that some comparable stimulus would be needed to push the U.S. economy onto a sustained upward course in the 1970s.* Without it, a policy aimed at raising the rate of surplus value might have little effect and indeed might make matters worse, since it would reduce consumption without holding out the prospect of the expanded markets which alone could justify an increase in capitalists' investment. Whether the editors of *Business Week* and those who think like them are aware that the policy they recommend (most people "doing with less so that big business

---

* This is of course not meant to imply that there will be no *cyclical* upturn in the visible future. As pointed out last month, the business cycle continues to operate whether the economy is buoyant or stagnant. Those who believe that the present recession/depression will "bottom out" by the end of 1975 and give way to an up phase of the cycle may therefore be right. But the fact that, at this writing, latest reports on inventories show them to be still rising (because sales are falling faster than production) would seem to suggest that it is not very likely the present slide will come to so early an end.

can have more") requires to be supplemented by applying a powerful stimulus to the economy is not clear. Our guess would be that they lack such awareness: conservative economic analysts always have a tendency to believe that the problem of markets will take care of itself (perhaps with a little help from monetary policy) if only workers can be put in their place. Since, as the whole history of capitalism shows, this is emphatically not the case, it follows that the policy proposals of conservatives are neither very interesting nor likely to be long persisted in if actually put into practice.*

Less doctrinaire bourgeois analysts, while not disagreeing about the importance of expanding the flow of surplus value, recognize that the present critical, and rapidly worsening, state of the economy calls for a far more comprehensive program. In this connection attention has recently centered on a proposal, emanating from various sources, to revive the Reconstruction Finance Corporation which was created in 1932, the last year of the Hoover administration, and liquidated in 1953 under Eisenhower.** The RFC was itself a revival of the War Finance

* The cases of Nixon and Ford are instructive in this connection. Both came out of the conservative wing of the Republican Party; each wanted to run his administration in accordance with the time-honored principles of Republican orthodoxy. But Nixon devalued the dollar, introduced price and wage controls, and became a "Keynesian" in matters of fiscal policy. Ford started out as a budget-balancer but soon changed his tune as the economy sank lower, and most recently has proposed a budget with the largest peace-time deficit in history. Both men became suspect to the true believers in their own party. It is of course not that either Nixon or Ford developed, or even tried to develop, an economic policy on any principles other than traditional conservatism; it is only that any attempt to practice traditional conservatism quickly results in fiasco.

** The proposal is not new, having been put forward by the chairmen of the Senate and House Banking Committees (Senator Sparkman and Representative Patman) as long ago as 1970 in the wake of the Penn Central bankruptcy and the near-panic it touched off. More recently a number of other Democratic leaders, including Senate Majority Leader Mike Mansfield, have endorsed the idea, and it was formally included in the program adopted at the Democrats' so-called mini-convention at Kansas City in early December. Among business leaders who have backed a revived RFC, in addition to Felix Rohatyn whose contribution is analyzed below, perhaps the most prominent is Alfred Hayes, president of the Federal Reserve Bank of New York.

Corporation established during the First World War to help finance munitions plants, a function which the RFC itself also performed during the Second World War. By far the most interesting and detailed blueprint for a new RFC which has come to our attention is contained in a lead article in the financial section of the Sunday *New York Times* of December 1, 1974, by Felix G. Rohatyn ("A New RFC Is Proposed for Business"). Rohatyn is an Austrian-born partner in the international investment banking firm of Lazard Frères, a director of several large corporations (including ITT), and reportedly a very shrewd operator in the politically sensitive field of corporate mergers. Inquiries directed to sources knowledgeable in Wall Street affairs have elicited the information that he is a registered Democrat and an adviser to Senator Henry Jackson of Washington, one of the front runners for the Democratic presidential nomination in 1976. Obviously he is a man whose pronouncements on economic policy should be taken seriously.

Rohatyn makes clear at the outset that he is interested in a revived RFC not merely as a salvage operation for financially troubled corporations but as a centerpiece for a much more far-reaching economic program. "If the RFC is to be recreated," he writes, "let it become a vital instrument of economic growth and not just another lender of last resort." What this means first and foremost is that the new RFC should have the power and the financial means (to be raised through the sale of government guaranteed bonds and notes) to provide large amounts of corporate equity, i.e., to buy freshly issued stock of corporations. The purpose would be threefold: first, to halt and reverse the trend so marked in recent years for corporate debt/equity ratios to deteriorate, with a consequent impairment of credit-worthiness and decline in stock prices (Rohatyn points out that in the last decade debt/equity ratios have risen from 25 percent to 40 percent); second, through such strengthening of corporate capital structures to enable the companies themselves to raise more money through sale of stocks rather than bonds; and third, to provide corporations with the wherewithal to undertake large projects needed for the viability of the capitalist system as a whole but insufficiently profitable to attract private investors. Rohatyn does not spell all this out in any detail, but he gives enough examples to indicate not only the sort of thing he has in mind but also some of the orders of magnitude which might be involved.

"The Big Board [i.e., the New York Stock Exchange] has recently estimated," he writes, "that the equity requirements of American industry for the foreseeable future could approximate $50 billion a year. It would appear that 1974 will produce only about $5 billion." If the revived RFC is supposed, directly and indirectly, to enable U.S. corporations to sell $40 billion or more annually in new stock issues, it is indeed being conceived of as a very major new component of U.S. capitalism.

But this is not the only function to be assigned to the new RFC:

> In addition to being an investor of last resort empowered to make equity infusions into banks or industrial enterprises deemed to be "in the public interest," the RFC could become a catalyst of stimulation in many areas. If a Manhattan-type project in the area of energy is ever undertaken, as is clearly required, the RFC could play a major role as an investor, risk-sharer, lender, and guarantor in a variety of projects. Although state regulated concerns such as utilities should perhaps not be eligible investments, the financing of massive generating facilities, the output of which could be shared by various grids, could be considered. Construction of over $20 billion worth of generating capacity has been canceled so far this year [1974], its effect to be felt years from now.

Furthermore, the RFC could step into messy situations which private enterprise has been incapable of straightening out —in Rohatyn's words, it "could facilitate major restructuring for the public purpose":

> For instance, if a merger of Pan American World Airways and Trans World Airlines appears to be nationally desirable, a $250-million equity investment in the merged company could accomplish much. It could cause the lenders of both corporations to convert some of their debt to equity, or reduce carrying charges, or stretch out maturities. It could ensure the merged company's ability to ride through the storm, achieve its savings and efficiencies, and ultimately be profitable enough to provide a fair return to the investors (including the RFC), a viable employer, and pass some savings on in lower fares.

Whatever it may have been thought of in its earlier incarnations, Rohatyn is emphatic that this time the RFC should become an integral feature of the system:

> The RFC should . . . become a permanent part of our economic establishment, not just as a last-ditch creditor but as a vibrant instrument of both rescue as well as stimulus. It need not, and should not, be a permanent investor in any one particular enterprise. It should only remain as an investor, either as a part-owner or creditor, until such time as it can, in the public interest, divest itself of the enterprise in which it invests and this investment is eligible for normal market channels or until the markets are capable of performing their function. The RFC therefore should, in effect, become a revolving fund—hopefully a profitable one—which steps in where no alternatives are available and which steps out when the public interest has been served and normal market forces can again operate.

Here again the seemingly casual mention of figures in the tens of billions of dollars for one industry and hundreds of millions for one company reveals the trend of the writer's thinking. And of course it would not be at all difficult to add to the list of projects which could use, and for the most part are not likely to be realized without, "an investor, risk-sharer, lender, and guarantor": rehabilitation of the railroads, urban mass transit, pollution control, low-cost housing, etc. Market-directed, profit-seeking private enterprise has failed miserably to meet even minimum (from the point of view of capitalism itself) social needs in these and other areas. What Felix Rohatyn is suggesting is that the capitalist class, acting through its state, should create a permanent institution capable of fulfilling the dual function of arresting the present potentially disastrous slide of the economy and subsidizing, directly or indirectly, investment in and production of goods and services which private monopolies consider too unprofitable and/or too risky to get into. If, by chance, some of these investments should turn out to be attractively profitable, they could and should be turned over to private hands: the state's job under capitalism is not to appropriate profits but to socialize losses and see that the system functions smoothly.

Rohatyn understands perfectly well that his proposals involve more than setting up a government corporation and providing it with money to invest. He brushes aside ideological objections—"socialism" from conservatives and "big business bail-outs" from the liberals—but he is quite willing to concede that the kind of RFC he has in mind can be effective only in a context of economic planning:

> There can be no denying that such an organization with the type of wide-ranging freedom described above, can be perceived as a first step toward state planning of the economy. Yet the time may have come for a public debate on this subject. . . . The premise that under [presently existing] circumstances, the country has to husband its resources more carefully, allocate them more prudently, and match its financial capabilities with its social priorities would appear to be worth considering. What many will call state planning would, to the average family, be no more than prudent budgeting.
>
> There are many who believe that long-range economic planning, at the federal level, will become a necessity. A plan without instruments to bring it to reality, however, is simply one more piece of paper. The RFC could be one of the key instruments in this kind of approach.

Rohatyn says nothing about what other key instruments of long-range economic planning might be necessary or desirable. But others are getting into the act, and it seems certain that from now on there will be no shortage of proposals and blueprints. A story in the March 10th issue of *Business Week* clearly points in this direction:

> Centralized government economic planning traditionally has been anathema to most businessmen, politicians, and economists. But with the economy in the worst slump since the 1930s, plus the added economic burden of the energy crisis, national planning is gaining new support in and out of Washington.
>
> A group of businessmen, labor leaders, and economists, headed by Nobel Prize-winning economist Wassily W. Leontieff, wants Congress to set up an office of National Economic Planning. The proposal, which is backed by such varied people as Robert V. Roosa, senior vice president of Brown Bros. Harriman & Co. [and former Under Secretary of the Treasury for Monetary Affairs], and Leonard Woodcock, president of the United Auto Workers, would give the planning office a broad mandate including:
>
> • Authority to collect and analyze detailed economic information from all sources both in the government and the private sector.
>
> • Responsibility for developing economic plans for periods of 5 to 15 years that are to be submitted to Congress and the President.

• Power to coordinate economic policy-making among such agencies as the Office of Management & Budget, the Treasury Dept., and the Council of Economic Advisers.

One other key instrument of long-range capitalist planning is likely to be some form of wage-and-price controls, often given the euphemistic name of "incomes policy," the real purpose of which is to regulate the rate of surplus value in the interests of capital. Such regulation is clearly implicit in the aim, cited above, of everyone else doing with less so that big business can have more, but its urgency is considerably less in a time of deepening depression than it was in the previous period of rampant inflation. Nevertheless, it occupies a central position in bourgeois planning literature (see, for example, J. K. Galbraith's latest book, *Economics and the Public Purpose*), and it is pretty sure to have a place in any planning scheme that may be adopted in the future.

Putting aside for the moment the question of the effectiveness of possible planning arrangements, we can say one thing with reasonable certainty: the present economic crisis and the renewed period of stagnation to which it is the prelude are bound to produce a great leap forward into state capitalism in the United States. This will take the form of extensive salvage operations which in fact are already under way in various sectors of the economy (banking, railroads, etc.). It is very likely to take the form of a massive government investment banking operation such as Rohatyn's RFC proposal. And it may involve more or less serious efforts at national economic planning. But whatever the mix, there can be no mistaking the powerful and clearly irreversible trend toward ever greater state intervention and participation in the U.S. economy.

Two brief comments are immediately in order. First, whatever conservatives and brainwashed social "scientists" may say, this has absolutely nothing to do with socialism.* Second, other

* Even Marxists sometimes tend to forget that socialism is not a mode of production *sui generis* but a transitional social formation, with the process of transition centering on the modification and eventual elimination of both capital and wage labor, i.e., the abolition of the oppressive, exploitative, and essentially alienating relationship between a separate class of owners/controllers of the means of production and workers forced

advanced capitalist countries are much further into state capitalism than the United States, so that what is starting to happen here can be looked upon as a catching-up process.

As to whether and/or to what extent the march to state capitalism can check the present crisis and alleviate the condition of stagnation which is now in prospect, one must evidently speak with considerable caution. We have already expressed the view that the government can prevent a full-blown panic by, in effect, assuming or guaranteeing the debts of threatened banks and corporations. How much more it can accomplish is the big question mark. A careful assessment of the experience of other countries in which state capitalism is more developed than in the United States would perhaps lead to the conclusion that something can be achieved in the way of propping up investment and employment, but not very much as long as they are dependent, as most of them are, on international developments beyond their control. But it would be wrong to transfer this conclusion directly to the United States, if only because the United States is by far the biggest member of the world capitalist system and hence plays a disproportionately large part in determining the international developments which bear so heavily on the others. It might be argued that if state capitalism in the United States could decisively improve the performance of this largest unit in the system, it would at the same time enable the others to reap the full potential benefits of state capitalism for themselves. Lacking any way to test the validity of this argument, we can only speculate on the first part of it, i.e., on how much state capitalism is likely to be able to accomplish here in this country.

And here, paradoxically (or at least so it will seem to many), the problem is much more a matter of politics than of economics. The enormous wealth and productivity of the United States confers on this country what, to use an analogy from mathematics, may be called almost unlimited degrees of economic freedom. *On paper* it should not be difficult to draw up

---

to sell their labor power to earn their livelihood. The bourgeois state always acts to strengthen and assure the continuation of this relationship, not to weaken or abolish it.

plans which, while remaining entirely within the framework of capitalism, would eliminate some of the system's almost incredibly wasteful and absurd irrationalities and mobilize the human and material resources thus made available to tackle many of the problems which now seem hopelessly insoluble. This is not the place to spin out such plans: that can safely be left to Professor Leontieff and his associates. Suffice it to say that actual experience during the Second World War proved that, starting from an unemployment situation somewhat similar to what we have today, it was possible to increase production by roughly 100 percent while at the same time drafting millions of men and women in the most productive age groups into the armed forces. *On paper* it should be possible to do even better today, with investment being channeled (perhaps by Felix Rohatyn's RFC) into developing new energy sources, rebuilding and extending the nation's rail network, providing the cities with modernized mass transport systems, de-polluting our air and water, furnishing halfway decent housing for perhaps 25 million families, etc., etc. This would certainly not have to involve any drastic redistribution of income or any crippling (to capitalism) reduction in the rate of surplus value: easily attainable increases in production could provide more all around.

It is precisely paper dreams of this kind that dazzle our well-intentioned planners. They forget to ask where all these incredibly wasteful and absurd irrationalities came from in the first place, and they overlook the stubborn fact that each and every one of them is the fortress or hiding place of vested interests which wield enormous political power and have absolutely no intention of making the least sacrifice for the common good, even if that somewhat elusive concept is defined wholly in capitalist terms. How is the energy problem to be approached, let alone solved, with the oil giants sitting astride an ever-increasing share of the nation's profitable energy sources and firmly in control of a large delegation of senators and representatives?*

---

* In the long run, which however may be said to have begun yesterday, the most rational solution to the energy problem is for the human race to learn to harness directly the flow of solar energy which reaches us uninterruptedly, absolutely free and in quantities which in a few days'

How are the railroads and urban mass transit going to get the priority which common sense tells us they deserve in the face of the vast power of the automobile, trucking, oil, and highway interests? Who is going to sell mass low-cost housing to the real estate and mortgage-banking interests? Give us persuasive answers to these questions and maybe we'll begin to pay more attention to your paper plans. But if you have no answers, please pardon us, there are more important matters to attend to.

The working class, defined broadly to include all those who need jobs as well as those who have them, is, as always, the special victim of capitalist depression. Real wages have been declining for several years now, and unemployment is far worse than the official figure of 8.2 percent (even officially it is over 40 percent for black teen-agers). Many workers are up to their ears in debt, unemployment benefits are rapidly running out, and huge numbers are being forced to go on welfare. Even those who still have jobs, knowing that their turn may come next, live in constant fear of ruin for themselves and their families. The working class in this the richest country in the world is quite literally facing a struggle for survival.

Under these circumstances, the unions, thoroughly bureaucratized, integrated into the system as a means of controlling workers rather than fighting for their interests, and in any case representing no more than about a quarter of the labor force, are not going to be magically transformed into effective instruments of working-class struggle. Their role today will probably be similar to that of the old A.F. of L. in the early 1930s, one of impotence and obstruction. And just as then, new organizations and new forms of struggle will doubtless emerge as workers are forced to face the grim realities of capitalist breakdown.

We do not pretend to be able to predict what these new organizations and forms of struggle will be or when they will begin to take shape. Our confidence that they will indeed emerge is based on the whole history of working-class move-

---

time far exceed the total amount of energy (largely the product of past and present solar radiation) stored in the earth's crust or growing on the earth's surface. How much enthusiasm are the oil companies and their minions likely to generate for *that* solution to the energy problem?

ments under capitalism: every major crisis releases dormant energies and stirs the working class to action, and there is no reason to believe it will be different this time.

In the meantime, we should be giving most careful consideration to what the role of radicals and revolutionaries should be in this new period which is now opening. As things stand in this country today, it would be foolish to imagine that they are in a position to give leadership and guidance to the coming struggles. If they are to earn the right to lead, they must first show that they understand both what is happening and the implications of what is happening. If and when they have achieved this understanding, they can begin to play a crucially important though initially modest role in the working-class movement: that of interpreter and teacher. They can make clear to increasing sectors of the working class the essentially *defensive* nature of the struggles they will be forced into. They can refuse to be drawn into, or to draw others into, the swamp of bourgeois reformism which is always ready to claim its victims. And above all they can hold high the banner of revolutionary socialism which in the final analysis holds out the only hope of a decent existence not only for American workers, but for all humanity threatened as never before with physical as well as spiritual destruction.

Capitalism and Unemployment

May 1975

At first glance it might seem that the labor supply or labor force is a very simple concept, and indeed this is the case in a rationally planned society, one in which the producers themselves are in control of what and for whom goods and services are to be provided. There the problem is obviously how to make best use of the ability and need to work of the *entire* population, due regard being paid to differences in age and physical capacity.

But when we turn our attention to a capitalist society, matters are very different. The problem is no longer what can be realistically accomplished with existing human and natural resources to satisfy the people's physical and spiritual needs. Rather it is what kind and size of labor force capital requires to maximize the production and realization of surplus value, and to this question there is no simple or unambiguous answer. About all that can be said with assurance is what Marx was the first to discover over a hundred years ago: "Capitalist production can by no means content itself with the quantity of disposable labor power which the natural increase of population yields. It requires for its free play an industrial reserve army independent of these natural limits." (*Capital*, Kerr ed., vol. 1, p. 696.) And in the same vein:

This article originally appeared in the June 1975 issue of *Monthly Review*.

> But if a surplus laboring population is a necessary product of accumulation or of the development of wealth on a capitalist basis, this surplus population becomes, conversely, the lever of capitalist accumulation, nay, a condition of existence of the capitalist mode of production. It forms an industrial reserve army that belongs to capital quite as absolutely as if the latter had bred it at its own cost. Independently of the limits of the actual increase of population, it creates for the changing needs of the self-expansion of capital a mass of human material always ready for exploitation. (*Ibid.*, p. 693)

Under these conditions, the labor force consists of two parts, the employed and the unemployed, with a gray area in between, containing the part-time or sporadically employed. Furthermore, all these categories of workers and potential workers continuously expand or contract with technological change, the ups and downs of the business cycle, and the vagaries of the market, all inherent characteristics of capitalist production. Thus the whole problem of the size and composition of the labor force under capitalism is in the nature of the case complicated and confusing; and to this must be added the fact that the official and unofficial spokesmen of capital have every interest in making it still more complicated and confusing in order to help conceal the frightful costs and irrationalities of a system of production for profit instead of production for use. In interpreting available data we therefore have the difficult task of trying to disentangle truth from material we know to be at best of doubtful accuracy and at worst riddled with distortion and deception.

The Deception of Averages

Official figures on unemployment, those issued in government press releases and reported in the newspapers, are mostly averages which are adjusted by statistical legerdemain for "seasonal" ups and downs in the number of job openings. Averages, however, can be very deceptive. Unemployed individuals are not averages, and the number of workers actually experiencing unemployment is significantly higher than the officially reported averages. In 1973, for example, the *average* number of employed was 84.4 million, while the number who *actually worked* all or part of the year was 100.2 million, i.e., almost 20 percent higher. The other side of the coin is that while the average unemployment rate in that year (near the top of a business-cycle upswing) was 4.9 percent, the proportion of workers experiencing one or more spells of unemployment during the year was no less than 14.2 percent! (*Manpower Report of the President, April 1975,* pp. 274, 276.) As will be explained presently, this figure is a gross underestimate, but even so it provides a dramatic illustration of how the form of presentation of statistics can obscure the content. The averages give an impression of a stable situation throughout the year, one described in the orthodox textbooks by the soothing term "equilibrium" (high-unemployment equilibrium, low-unemployment equilibrium, etc.). The data on individual workers' experience, on the contrary, shows us a moving picture of continuous violent expansions and contractions in both the employed and the unemployed segments of the labor force.

Further evidence on the real nature of employment under capitalism is provided by more detailed data on the work experience of persons 16 years of age and over during 1973, near the peak of a period of capitalist prosperity. Taking all the people who worked for some time during that year, we find that only 57 percent had year-round, full-time jobs (defined as those who worked at least 50 weeks during the year at the same place of employment). It is natural that this percentage should be less than 100 percent. We know, for example, that about 15 percent of those employed voluntarily worked part-time. In addition, some turnover is to be expected as a result of retirement at old age, illness, and voluntary job changes. Yet these reasons could hardly account for the fact that as much as 43 percent of the working force was not employed at year-round full-time jobs. This becomes clearer if we compare work experience in different industries, since turnover due to such reasons as retirement and illness should be pretty much the same in most industries. (See Table 1, p. 80.)

That these relatively low percentages are due to lack of year-round jobs rather than to idiosyncrasies of workers can be seen from the relatively high percentages in some sub-groups not shown in Table 1. In the categories "other public utilities" (largely electric power) and "chemicals and allied products," over 80 percent of the work force was employed year-round, while in "automobiles," "primary metal industries," and "railroads and railway express," the percentages ranged between 75 and 80. But for the working population as a whole, as already noted, only 57 percent had year-round jobs. Of the remaining 43 percent, to repeat, some worked part-time because they preferred to (but not necessarily because they didn't need full-time jobs, as in the case of working mothers who had no day-care centers available), others retired (not all because they wanted to or could afford to, but because of lack of job opportunities for older workers), while some dropped out because of illness.* But for many, if not most, of the non-full-timers their life was one of hopping from one job to another, including one or more periods of unemployment during the year.

All this is of course the inevitable product of a social system geared not to the satisfaction of the *needs* of people but to the *use* of people for the aggrandizement of capital. In Marx's words, quoted above, capitalism "creates for the changing needs of the self-expansion of capital a mass of human material always ready for exploitation." Ignoring this most fundamental

TABLE I

Selected Industries	*Percent of Wage and Salary Earners in Each Industry Who Worked Year Round at Full-time Jobs in 1973*
Agriculture	46.8%
Construction	51.1
Manufacturing	68.9
Transportation and Public Utilities	73.0
Retail Trade	38.9
Finance and Services	62.1

Source: *Manpower Report of the President, April 1975* (Washington, D.C.: U.S. Government Printing Office), p. 275.

* A number of those who dropped out because of illness may also represent a form of unemployment resulting from work experience. As reported in the *New York Times,* May 12, 1975, a federally financed medical survey found that diseases suffered by three out of every ten workers were caused by work conditions. This is a minimum estimate based on those diseases that can unquestionably be identified as occupationally induced.

characteristic of the society they are supposedly analyzing, bourgeois economists and statisticians proceed on the implicit assumption that irregularities in employment are part of the God-given order of nature which must be eliminated by such statistical devices as averaging and seasonal adjustments in order to get at the "true" level of unemployment.* In this way they hide the grim facts of the capitalist labor market: that for a large number of workers only temporary, intermittent, and insecure jobs are ever provided; and on the other hand that private enterprise depends on always having a large reserve of labor available to supply its needs when demand is brisk, to be discarded promptly when demand slackens off.

Overestimating the Number of Employed

There are two ways in which official labor-force statistics systematically overestimate the amount of employment. The first has to do with the treatment of part-time work. In current estimates of employment, for example, some four million workers are included who on the average work about half a week, not because they want to but because they cannot get full-time jobs. (U.S. Department of Labor, *Employment and Earnings*, April 1975, p. 37.) This is equivalent to 1.7 million full-time unemployed. (See Table 3, p. 87.)

The second systematic overestimate of employment relates to the inclusion of unpaid family workers. Government data show that in 1973 there were over 700,000 unpaid family workers in agriculture and over 900,000 in nonagricultural enterprises. (*Manpower Report of the President, op. cit.*, p. 274.) Some of these are doubtless in the "unpaid family worker" category not because they are really receiving no compensation for their labor but because of the way the family in a male-

---

* It is also routinely assumed that a substantial amount of unemployment is "normal," in the sense of being necessary to contain inflation and keep the system on an even keel. Twenty-five years ago most economists would have put this "norm" in the three to four percent range. Nowadays it would be more like five to six percent, and it will doubtless drift upward as the economy sinks deeper and deeper into stagnation. By the end of the decade of the 1970s it may well be that "full employment" will be defined as 10 percent unemployment.

dominated society receives and distributes its income. But it is no less reasonable to assume that a significant portion of these people are really what are usually called "disguised unemployed," i.e., people who are unable to find a job and eke out a livelihood through shining shoes, selling matches, etc. An alternative possibility in some cases is to help out on the family farm or in the family store, sharing in what is usually already the meager family income.

The Subemployed

Closely related to the disguised unemployed is another much larger category of workers who may be called the "subemployed," i.e., workers who are employed at wages below, and often much below, the "official poverty line" (in Marxian terminology, workers whose wages are less than the value of their labor power). This poverty line was placed by the Social Security Administration in 1970 at $4,200 a year for a family of four. Yet in 1972, two years later, there were no fewer than six million full-time workers counted in the official statistics who earned less than two dollars an hour, which means that if they worked 40 hours a week for 50 weeks they would earn less than $4,000. These six million workers were clearly below the poverty line (especially considering the rise in prices between 1970 and 1972) and many were far below it.* Doubtless many of these people could without unduly stretching the concept be included in the disguised unemployment category; and yet for the great majority, so classifying them would be misleading. They are employed in the full sense of the term, i.e., they are workers who receive wages and produce surplus value, and as a group they constitute a permanent part of the labor force. Above all, and unlike the disguised unemployed, from

* On this and other aspects of sub- and underemployment, see the valuable article by Thomas Vietorisz, Robert Mier, and Benjamin Harrison, "Full Employment at Living Wages" in *The Annals,* March 1975. It should be added that the six million figure is by no means a measure of the total number of people living below the poverty line, since it does not take into account poverty among part-time workers, retired persons, the unemployed, the disabled, the self-employed, those on welfare rolls, etc.

the point of view of capital they are absolutely indispensable for the very existence of a huge number of capitalist enterprises which in the aggregate play an important part in the functioning of the capitalist economy. The extent of this importance can in no way be measured by their own income or by that of their employers, many of whom are petty capitalists who themselves live little if any better than workers. For what has to be kept constantly in mind is that these workers are employed in highly competitive branches of an increasingly monopoly-dominated economy. The result is that a large part, and perhaps most (there is no way of measuring), of the surplus value *produced* in these competitive industries is *drained off* and *realized* in the monopolized sectors of the economy. Nor is this the only reason why this substandard and superexploited part of the economy is important to big capital. The existence of a large number of low-wage workers who are always ready and anxious to move into better-paying jobs if any are available acts as a drag on the bargaining power of the better-paid workers in the monopolized sectors of the system. In this sense the subemployed, without ceasing to be part of the active labor army, function as part of the reserve army or the relative surplus population of which Marx said: "Relative surplus population is . . . the pivot on which the law of supply and demand of labor works. It confines the field of action of this law within the limits absolutely convenient to the activity of exploitation and to the domination of capital." (*Capital, op. cit.*, p. 701.)

Underestimating the Size of the Labor Force

The converse of the overestimates of employment which were discussed above is the minimization of the size of the labor force. While at first glance it might seem that a statistical measure of the labor force would have independent and objective validity, the fact is that it is a statistical construct into which enter many subjective elements and value judgments in the various stages in the process of construction. And here the narrow and timid outlook of the specialists blends with the practical politics of the policy-makers who fear the implications of a true measure of the volume of unemployment. What results is the strange and ironic phenomenon of a declining labor force precisely when more workers lose jobs and the recession deepens. Thus, an article in the *New York Times* of March 9th, headlined "The Labor Force is Shrinking Drastically," reports with a straight face:

> The Federal Government's latest figures show unemployment unchanged for the first time in months. . . . There was a decline of 540,000 in the number of people at work in February, but the unemployment rate remained static because about 580,000 already jobless persons stopped looking for work last month, in many cases because they felt there were no jobs to be found. Thus the government did not count them statistically as unemployed.

This sort of statistical sleight-of-hand is not always as successful in concealing the growth of unemployment as it was for last February, but it has worked over the years to obfuscate the measurement of the labor force and hence the number of unemployed. The key is the use of a restricted definition of unemployment, as can be seen from the following description of how the numbers are derived. The official government estimates of unemployment are compiled from monthly investigations of a sizable sample of families around the nation (the Current Population Survey). Field investigators question a representative of each family studied (usually the adult found at home) about the employment status of each member of the family 16 years of age and over. Based on the answers given to the investigator, each member of the family counted is classified into one of three groups: employed, unemployed, or not in the labor force. (The sum of the first two, the employed and the unemployed, is the labor force estimate.)

The decision as to who should be classified as employed is pretty clear-cut, apart of course from the built-in biases, some of which were discussed above. But the separation of the remainder between "unemployed" and "not in the labor force" raises many thorny problems, especially in view of the way a capitalist economy generates alternating expansions and contractions of the labor market and capital's ever-present need to maintain an adequate labor reserve. The solution chosen by the government specialists is to count as in the labor force only those who are actually employed or are reported as having engaged in a specific job-seeking activity during the four weeks preceding the time of the survey. And all those who are not employed or who have not recently looked for a job (including those who have not looked because they know very well that jobs are not to be had) are by this definition not in the labor force. Using this method, the Current Population Survey conducted in April of this year reached the conclusion that 8.2 million persons were unemployed. This represented 8.9 percent of the official labor force—the highest reported rate since 1941, when it averaged 9.9 percent for the year as a whole.*

How Many Really Unemployed?

When one probes more deeply into the underlying data of the Current Population Survey, however, it is not difficult to discover how inadequate the current estimates of average unemployment are (leaving aside here the question discussed above about the difference between averages and individuals). What we discover is that among the people labelled "not in the labor force" in the first quarter of 1975—and hence not counted as unemployed—there are over 5 million persons who answered "yes" when asked: do you want a regular, full- or part-time job *now*? These 5 million (or members of their families who answered for them) were then asked the reasons for not looking for work. The classification of the reasons is given in Table 2 (p. 86).

The 1.1 million who were not looking for a job because they didn't think they could get one (line 4 of Table 2) are often referred to as "discouraged workers." It is hard to

---

* Fuller material on current techniques for measuring the labor supply, as well as an excellent critical examination of these methods and their implications, is to be found in the March 1975 issue of *The Annals* devoted to "Planning for Full Employment." In addition to the article cited in the preceding footnote, the following articles from the same issue of *The Annals* are worthy of careful consideration: Bertram M. Gross and Jeffrey D. Straussman, " 'Full' Employment Growthmanship and the Expansion of the Labor Supply"; Stanley Moses, "Labor Supply Concepts: The Political Economy of Conceptual Change"; and Frank F. Furstenberg, Jr. and Charles A. Thrall, "Counting the Jobless: The Impact of Job Rationing on the Measurement of Unemployment."

TABLE 2

Reasons for Not Looking for a Job	*First Quarter 1975 (in millions)*
School Attendance	1.5
Ill Health, Disability	0.7
Home Responsibilities	1.2
Think Cannot Get Job	1.1
Other Reasons	0.8
	—
Total Persons Not Included in Labor Force but Who Want a Job Now	5.3

Source: *Employment and Earnings,* April 1975 (Washington, D.C.: U.S. Department of Labor), p. 57.

figure out by what rules of reason these persons are not to be considered unemployed. And surely many others, if not all, of those who specifically said they wanted a job *now* are in truth unemployed. Among those reported to be at school (which includes vocational training) are many who went back to school precisely because they could not find a job, as well as others who are finishing their scheduled education but who need the income from full- or part-time employment.

One might assume that ill heath and disability are sufficient reasons for not being included in the labor force. Why then do 700,000 in this category say they want a job now? Could it not be that among them are disabled persons able to perform productively but who are not seeking work because jobs are scarce and employers discriminate against them? Could it not also be that in this category are people who are ill or recuperating from illness, which is why they did not actively beat the bushes in the labor market, but who nevertheless currently want and need jobs?

The next line of Table 2 (people who want a job but are not looking because of home responsibilities) consists almost entirely of women. And they probably fall into two groups: those with young children at home and those with an ailing adult in the family needing attention. Here the absence of day-care centers and the lack of visiting nurses are the problem. But are the individuals who want a job but are prevented from seeking one because of insufficient social services any the less unemployed?

Although there are many areas of possible doubt about the exact status of these more than 5 million job-wanters excluded from the unemployment count, it is still possible to use these data to arrive at an approximation of a more meaningful estimate of the current volume of unemployment: we need only approach the problem in a conservative way. With this in mind let us exclude all those who want a job but say they are in school and those who report ill health and disability. However, we will include in the estimate of unemployment those who want a job but are not looking because of home responsibilities, those who believe they cannot get a job, and the "all other" catch-all category. In addition, we will add to the unemployed the full-time equivalent of those workers who wanted to work full-time but could find only part-time work. And we will make no other adjustment for the overestimates of employment discussed above. Using this compromise (and we believe very cautious) approach, we arrive at the following estimate of unemployment for April of this year:

TABLE 3

	Millions
(1) Officially reported unemployment	8.2
(2) Persons wanting a job, but not included in the official count of unemployment[a]	3.1
(3) Adjustment for those involuntarily working part-time[b]	1.7
Total unemployment	13.0

(a) Excludes those wanting a job, but who reported that they were not actively looking for work because they were at school or ill. These data are for the first quarter of 1975, the latest date for which this information is available. In the light of recent trends, however, this is most likely an underestimate of the situation in April 1975.

(b) The full-time equivalent unemployment of those working part-time (an average of 22.5 hours a week) but who want full-time work (40 hours a week).

If, for purposes of comparability, we add line (2) of Table 3 to the official labor force estimate, we find that the 13 million represent a more realistic *13.6 percent of the labor* *force unemployed* instead of the official 8.9 percent. And it should be stressed that the 13.6 percent is still an understatement, due to the conservative nature of the assumptions we made.*

The Outlook for the Next Decade

The data on employment and unemployment, if understood properly, reveal an important phase, yet hardly the only one, of the failure of U.S. capitalism. We have seen, on the one hand, the extent of job insecurity even at the peak of prosperity, and, on the other hand, how much the volume of unemployment has grown at this stage of the recession. It is equally important to understand that this failure to provide jobs and job security is hardly likely to evaporate. On the contrary, all indications are that it is going to get worse in the years ahead.

In the two previous chapters we discussed at length current trends in the U.S. economy, presenting reasons for believing that the country is once again entering a period of stagnation comparable to that of the 1930s. Our purpose here is not to repeat what was said earlier but simply to demonstrate how powerfully existing and projected labor-force statistics buttress this conclusion. We ask how many net new jobs would be needed between now and 1985 (1) to reduce unemployment from the above estimated 13.6 percent of the labor force to 5 percent (using the same methods of estimation)—reducing the actual number of unemployed from 13.0 million to 4.8 million; (2) to provide jobs for the normal increase in population, again assuming 5 percent unemployment; and (3) to provide jobs needed to replace those lost owing to increasing labor productivity (assuming that output per man-hour will continue to grow at the same not very high rate of the last

---

* It is interesting to note that this estimate of real unemployment is an increase of 52.8 percent over the official rate, and that back in 1971 in this space we estimated real as compared to official unemployment at the end of 1970 by an entirely different method and came out with the conclusion that the real rate was 51.6 percent higher than the official. See "Economic Stagnation and Stagnation of Economics," *Monthly Review*, April 1971, especially pp. 3-6.

ten years). Here are the estimates (see Technical Note):

TABLE 4

	Number of Net New Jobs Needed 1975-1985 (in millions)
(1) To reduce the current unemployment rate to 5 percent	8.2
(2) To accommodate population increase, assuming same 5 percent unemployment rate	15.0
(3) To compensate for productivity gains	12.8
Total	36.0

Our estimates thus indicate that for unemployment in 1985 to drop to somewhere near the average of the past 25 years (the official average during those years was 4.8 percent), no fewer than 36 million jobs would have to be created.

Compare this with how many jobs *actually were* created in the last ten years—years which already are being looked back upon as a period of extraordinary prosperity. According to the latest *Manpower Report of the President,* the number is 16.6 million. This is about 46 percent of what would be needed for U.S. capitalism to function in the next decade approximately as well as it has in the post-Second World War period.

Further comment seems superfluous.

TECHNICAL NOTE

Method of estimating the number of additional jobs needed over the next ten years, as given in the above tabulation:

Line (1). Adding the underestimate of 3.1 million (line 2 of Table 3) to the officially reported 92.3, we arrive at an adjusted estimate of 95.4 million in the labor force, or 63.3 percent of the current population 16 years of age and over. Thus, 8.2 million new jobs would be needed to bring unemployment down to 4.8 million, or 5 percent of the adjusted labor force.

Line (2). According to the *Manpower Report of the President, op. cit.,* p. 309, there will be 175.7 million persons 16 years of age and over in 1985, or an increase of 24.9 million over the current level. If the percent of the population in the labor force will be the same as estimated in (1) above, this will mean a 15.8 million increase in the labor force by 1985. Assuming that 5 percent of these will be unemployed, 15 million new jobs will thus be needed to accommodate the population increase.

Line (3). Output per man-hour in the private economy increased by 22.6 percent between 1964 and 1974 (calculated from data in the *Manpower Report of the President, op. cit.,* p. 336). We assumed that man-hours per week will not change in the next ten years, and that the average rate of productivity increase will be the same as in the past decade. Applying this to only those currently employed in the private economy (69.3 out of the total 84.1 million employed in April 1975, the remainder having government jobs), we find that the number of jobs in the private economy would decline to 56.5 million if production remained constant. Thus, production would have to increase sufficiently to supply 12.8 million jobs to compensate for those lost due to the expected decline in the demand for labor resulting from steadily rising productivity.

Capital Shortage: Fact and Fancy

February 1976

One of the great ironies of our time is that precisely when all signs point to an overproduction of capital, a great hue and cry is being raised over an alleged shortage of capital. At least 25 percent of manufacturing capacity is standing idle (in some industries unused capacity is over 35 percent), residential construction is down 50 percent from its previous (1972) high, and there are far more unemployed than would be needed to operate the idle plants and machinery and to build new homes. Yet in the midst of the most severe economic decline since the Great Depression the business community and bourgeois economists are zeroing in on capital insufficiency as the most crucial problem facing U.S. capitalism. Here are some of the outcroppings of this new ideological departure.

(1) In the fall of 1974 the New York Stock Exchange issued, to the accompaniment of considerable fanfare, a scholarly-type report purporting to demonstrate that "a capital shortage is no longer a threat for the future, but a fact of the present." The Exchange statisticians calculated that while \$4.7 trillion of capital will probably be needed during the coming decade, the expected supply of funds for investment from savings of business firms and individuals would amount to only \$4.05 trillion, leaving an estimated capital gap of \$650 billion.

This article originally appeared in the April 1976 issue of *Monthly Review*.

(2) The research department of the Chase Manhattan Bank, using somewhat different estimates, arrived at substantially the same disturbing conclusion. The study provided the meat for repeated full-page advertisements in the *Wall Street Journal.* Under a scare headline crying "Wolf!", Chase Manhattan warned: "We've got to build considerably more in the next ten years than we've got standing right now."

(3) ITT fell in line with the mounting clamor by proclaiming in a *Wall Street Journal* advertisement: "What happens to Capitalism if we run out of Capital? In boardrooms and treasurers' offices across the U.S. that's Topic A today."

(4) Academic and private research organization economists were not far behind in exploring the anxieties in the house of capitalism.* They warmed up their computers, gazed into crystal balls, and issued ponderous reports, concluding that the problem might not be as dire as the business community predicted. Their statistical projections showed that enough capital would probably be generated in the next ten years to meet energy needs, overcome purported shortages in raw materials processing industries, install pollution abatement equipment, as well as cope with housing and mass transportation requirements. But to achieve these goals an increased percentage of the nation's output would have to be devoted to capital investment. Thus even though the learned economists look down their noses at the alarums of the business world, they reach substantially the same conclusion: there must be a leap forward in spending for capital goods.

(5) The U.S. Department of Commerce prepared a detailed study of capital requirements, this one being limited to the remainder of the decade. The Commerce study, as reported in the 1976 *Annual Report to Congress* of the President's Council of Economic Advisers, wound up with a conclusion that was qualitatively consistent with the results of studies

* For example: Barry Bosworth, James S. Duesenberry, and Andrew S. Carron, *Capital Needs in the Seventies* (Washington, D.C.: The Brookings Institution, 1975); and Allen Sinai and Roger Brinner, *The "Capital Shortage": Near-Term Outlook and Long-Term Prospects* (a "Special Study" incorporated in the Summer 1975 Forecast distributed to clients of Data Resources, Inc.)

attained by business and private economists. The ratio of business fixed investment to gross national product, the study states, "may have to average 12 percent from 1975 to 1980 to meet the capital requirements projected for 1980"—a significant increase from the 10.4 percent level of the preceding decade.

(6) *Business Week* devoted a special section of its September 22, 1975, issue to what it termed "The Capital Crisis," along with a subhead about the "$4 trillion America needs to grow." Candid as usual with its business readers, *Business Week* succinctly pointed out what this hullabaloo is all about: if a larger share of the national output is to be used for capital investment, then a smaller share will be available for consumption. Closing the presumed gap between the supply and demand for capital, it was explained, "at a minimum requires changes in the tax structure that would provide greater incentives for savings and investment and greater disincentives for consumption."

Before we get into a more substantial evaluation of this fuss and fury over a supposed capital inadequacy, the underlying weakness of the various projections of capital supply and demand should be noted. Above all, the very attempt to make long-term estimates of needs and resources flies in the face of the inherently anarchic nature of the capitalist economy. Decisions about investment and production are made by separate individuals and corporations in the midst of constantly changing and unpredictable market conditions at home and abroad. Of necessity, forecasting can only be a guessing game in which economists and statisticians play with numbers and juggle assumptions not only about innumerable economic developments and trends but also about future policies of governments, domestic and foreign. Since changes in the short run are sometimes relatively small, the margin of forecasting error for, say, three to six months can now and then be fairly minor—although professional forecasters have as yet hardly established a trustworthy track record for even such limited projections. Detailed estimates for all areas of the economy over a decade in the future, on the other hand, can only be considered speculation pure and simple.

Since the total unreliability of long-range economic forecasts has been demonstrated time and again and is by now obvious to everyone with eyes to see, we have to ask what real purpose they serve. And the only possible answer is that they represent a desperate effort to conceal, or perhaps in some cases wish away, infirmities in the business and banking systems —infirmities, be it noted, which the forecasting fraternity signally failed to foresee. For what we are dealing with is not what *Business Week* calls a "capital crisis," but rather a crisis of capitalism.

In examining the issues at stake we need to keep clearly in mind the distinction between *physical* and *money* capital. It is hardly surprising that money capital should be tight during some phases of the business cycle, and especially in a period when inflation is the order of the day, public and private debt are rapidly growing, and speculation is rampant. But a money-capital stringency is a very different matter from an inadequacy of real capital, or capital goods. An outstanding feature of the U.S. economy has long been an ability rapidly to expand its productive capacity. Through mastery of the machine-building processes, this country's industry has the essential ingredients for flexible self-expansion. Above all it possesses an enormous capacity to enlarge the stock of basic machine tools and other factory equipment that can be used to make still more capital goods which in turn can be applied to the mass production of consumer goods, public utility and transportation facilities, and construction materials.

Ample evidence of this phenomenal ability to make capital goods in a hurry piled up during the relatively few years of U.S. participation in the Second World War. This can best be appreciated against the background of the preceding Great Depression. Let us therefore look at some of the highlights of the decline and weak recovery of the 1930s (Table 1, p. 95).

For our present purpose we want to call attention to the listless recovery of investment. The 1920s witnessed an over-production of capital goods relative to the effective domestic and foreign demand. Resulting cutbacks between 1929 and 1933 were drastic indeed, amounting, as can be seen in Table

TABLE I

Consumption and Investment
1929 = 100

	Personal Consumption Expenditures for Goods	*Investment in Plant and Equipment*	*Investment in Housing*
1929	100.0	100.0	100.0
1933	78.2	28.7	20.2
1939	111.8	57.7	78.8

Source: *The National Income and Product Accounts of the United States, 1929-65* (Washington, D.C.: U.S. Department of Commerce, 1966), p. 4. The data are part of the gross national product accounts, adjusted for changes in prices, and converted to relatives with 1929 as a base.

1, to more than 70 percent in plant and equipment and 80 percent in home-building. Quite a few of the machine-tool builders—the producers of machines used to make other machines and manufacturing equipment—all but closed their doors for months at a time during the depressed thirties. In industry after industry, depreciated capital stock was not replaced during most of the decade. The consequence was that even during the recovery period, from 1933 on, capital spending lagged far behind consumer purchases. By 1939 consumer demand, bolstered by various New Deal measures, stood at 12 percent above the previous prosperity peak. (This was only partly a rise in per capita consumption, since there had meanwhile been an increase of population of slightly over 7 percent.) Yet, despite the growth of consumption demand, investment had still increased to less than 60 percent of the 1929 level in the case of plant and equipment and less than 80 percent in home-building.

In these circumstances one might well have expected the tocsin to be sounded about capital shortages. After all, wasn't more capital needed to put to work the more than 17 percent of the labor force still unemployed, bring up to snuff the deteriorating and aging capital stock, and provide sorely needed housing? But clearly at that time there was no shortage of capital *from the capitalists' point of view.* Quite the contrary. Interest rates were at or near an all-time low: in 1939 the rate on three-month treasury bills was .023 percent and on top-rated corporate bonds 3.01 percent. Any credit-worthy borrower could easily have raised almost unlimited amounts of capital—provided, of course, there were profitable projects to spend it on. What stood in the way, therefore, was not a capital shortage but a lack of profitable investment opportunities. So the economy stagnated throughout a whole decade, with unemployment averaging more than 18 percent, idle capacity more than a third of total capacity, and the country's physical means of production aging and declining in efficiency.

In spite of this dismal record, however, it was soon to become crystal clear that the U.S. economy retained a fantastic capability for rapid self-expansion. The turnabout in real capital supply came with the outbreak of the Second World War. France and England ordered large quantities of machinery to build up their munitions-producing capacity. The United States, in turn, started an energetic program to build its own war potential, and began, under the Lend-Lease program, to produce and ship war equipment for its future allies. All this renewed business activity generated an upsurge in jobs and wages, and produced a strong advance in consumer demand.

Now, look at what happened in two strategic areas, the machinery and transportation-equipment industries (Table 2, p. 97). The sick machinery industry came back to life in only one year—advancing more than 30 percent in 1940 to surpass its previous peak in 1929.* But this sort of leap forward was only a first step in startling growth. From the record high point reached in 1940, machinery output pushed ahead by 62 percent in 1941, and continued to advance at a rate of 54 and 30 percent respectively in the first two full years of U.S. participation in the war. In three years, 1941-1943, U.S. manufacturers of these capital goods reached a level of output more than three times that of the previous high.

An even more dramatic picture presents itself in the transportation-equipment industry, which includes autos, trucks, airplanes, ships, tanks, and railroad equipment. Here we find

---

* There is no contradiction in the fact that 1939 machinery output as shown in Table 2 was relatively higher than the same year's investment in plant and equipment as presented in Table 1. The latter was especially depressed because of a particularly low level of new plant construction.

TABLE 2
Production of Machinery and Transportation Equipment
1929 = 100

	Machinery	*Transportation Equipment*
1929	100	100
1939	80	108
1940	105	183
1941	170	346
1942	262	549
1943	341	537

Source: Board of Governors of the Federal Reserve System, *Revision of Industrial Production Index,* October 1943. The Federal Reserve Board computed these production indexes on a 1935-39 basis. These have been converted for this table to a 1929 basis.

that even though by 1939 the industry had already exceeded the former 1929 peak, production went up almost 70 percent in 1940, and by 1942 was more than five times that of 1929.

Such a miraculous production record involved of course a great deal of government intervention: guaranteeing handsome profits to corporations, shutting down for the duration of the war such activities as auto production and home-building for civilians, and establishing priorities for the use of scarce materials and components. Still, it should also be remembered that a good deal of the fantastic output of both of these major industries entailed designing and tooling up for new and challenging products. The machinery industry had to produce, among other things, an abundance of equipment that could handle the forming, shaping, and cutting of large-size and thick steel plates for tanks and warships, as well as the vast amount of specialized work needed for making the aluminum bodies and the engines for airplanes. The various transportation-equipment enterprises had to learn almost overnight to mass-produce merchant and war ships, tanks, airplanes, and heavy artillery carriers.

We chose to highlight these two industries because they are major centers of actual and potential capital goods manufactures. The heights they reached naturally called for coordinated increases in the output of many other products, as, for example, raw materials and electric power. It is important to understand that the astounding rates of increase shown here and those that also occurred in accompanying industries are not statistical idiosyncrasies, such as one might get by measuring recovery rates of increase from depression lows. The accelerated growth discussed here is relative to previous peaks of achievement. This could only have been realized by increasing the utilization of existing capacity, notably by adding shifts, and by a furious rate of building entirely new capacity. All this, remember, was carried out starting with plant and equipment that had been gathering rust and dust during the many years of depression and stagnation.

The history of war production thus demonstrates with crystal clarity that, as far as *real* capital is concerned, talk about a capital shortage is sheer nonsense. Not only does the United States economy have the latent ability to generate an enormous amount of new capacity, but it can fabricate a great deal more with just the existing capacity.* If the standards for getting more production used during the Second World War were applied today, we would probably find that only 50 percent, or maybe less, of existing manufacturing capacity is being used—instead of the official 75-percent figure based on current operating practices.

Matters stand entirely differently if we move from issues of *real* capital (and social needs) to the world of capitalist finance. Only then can the possibility of capital shortage be taken seriously. Here of course we become involved with the limitations of the capitalist economy, and more specifically with barriers to capitalist development that arise from the stagnation tendencies inherent in monopoly capital. The effort to maintain the flow of profits in a period of unfolding of stagnation has inevitably

* In this connection it is pertinent to point out that the potential increase today is relatively much greater than it was to the outbreak of the Second World War. In the earlier period, as we have stressed, capital stock had been allowed to age and degenerate. In the last three decades, by contrast, the capital stock has grown more or less steadily and its average age has declined. It has been estimated by John C. Musgrave (*Survey of Current Business,* March 1974) that the average age of the gross stock of manufacturing plant and equipment went down from 13.4 years in 1939 to 9 years in 1973, a decline of over 30 percent.

led to greater and greater reliance on inflation, speculation, and debt expansion. And these in turn throw up major obstacles to further capitalist growth because they increasingly threaten the financial stability and viability of capitalist enterprise. And it is this structural weakness, not social concern about pollution of the environment or meeting the needs of the people, that provokes the furor over capital shortage. A *Wall Street Journal* article pinpoints the problem with respect to banking, as seen by money-market experts:

> At the heart of the potential trouble, these specialists say, is the inadequate capital structure supporting the banking network. That structure has been stretched thin through years of boom demand for loans; during that time, banks have been balancing burgeoning assets on an only modestly expanding capital base. Specialists in the banking industry believe that this imbalance perhaps has been pushed about as far as it can go. And with the failure of several large banks in recent years, banks and their regulators have become increasingly worried that any further erosion of capital positions could seriously undermine investor and depositor confidence in the banking industry. (June 13, 1975)

And the Council of Economic Advisers, though expressing itself in gingerly fashion, as befits a policy-making government agency, is quite frank in presenting its view of the causes of the business difficulties by highlighting the dangers associated with inflation and debt:

> The increase in debt-equity ratios during recent years has made business more vulnerable to the vicissitudes of the credit market and to unanticipated changes in the rates of inflation and profits. The tax treatment of interest payments as a deductible business expense makes debt financing particularly attractive when inflation premiums are included in interest rates. Nonetheless, debt-equity ratios have probably reached higher levels than firms would like to maintain under present conditions. While unanticipated increases in the rate of inflation have lowered the real cost of amortizing old debt, this gain has not been reflected in a higher valuation of corporate equities in periods of rising inflation. The resulting unfavorable structure of business liabilities may have created some structural financing problems, and it may have increased default risks, the costs of financing, and the cutoff rate of return on new projects. (*Economic Report of the President,* Washington, D.C., Government Printing Office, January 1976, p. 40)

A few facts will demonstrate that structural strains have indeed, and not "may have" as the Council of Economic Advisers puts it, emerged. Look first at Table 3, which shows how nonfinancial corporations have been getting the funds they need, other than from profits generated internally.

TABLE 3
Sources of External Financing
Nonfinancial Corporations

	(1) *Sale of Stock*	*(2)* *Long-term Debt*[a]	*(3)* *Short-term Debt*[b]	*(4)* *Total External Financing*
		(Percentages)		
1950-54	22.7	55.7	21.6	100
1955-59	18.0	55.5	26.5	100
1960-64	7.6	63.2	29.2	100
1965-69	4.7	53.3	42.0	100
1970-74	13.9	50.1	36.0	100

(a) Bonds and mortgages.

(b) Bank loans, commercial paper, acceptances, finance company loans, and U.S. government loans.

Source: Calculated from Flow of Funds Accounts given in *Federal Reserve Bulletin,* various issues.

Two things are especially noteworthy here: (1) the relatively small proportion of new financing that comes from the sale of stocks, and the concomitant reliance on debt instruments; (2) the large and growing share of short-term debt in the total. According to the best advice found in economics textbooks and to the platitudes of the business community, the soundest and most trustworthy source of external financing should be the stock market. Profit, so the experts say, is the reward for risk-taking, and it is the willingness of capitalists to invest in risky enterprises that supplies the motive power for economic growth. Conversely, corporations will be on a firmer basis to the extent that they rely on equity capital, which does not have to be repaid, instead of on borrowing. Yet the picture for the last 25 years is at sharp variance with the conventional wisdom. At a minimum, during 1950-1954, corporations got roughly 77 percent of their outside money capital by going into debt, while during the years 1965-1969 they obtained about 95 percent of their external funds in this way. Even when some stabs were made at going back to the stock market for capital, as in the boom stock-market years of the early 1970s, the sale of equity securities accounted for only 14 percent of outside capital.

While corporate executives have been unwilling or unable to resort to the stock market as a source of outside funds, the bond market has developed special attractions for them. Interest payments are tax deductible. Hence as long as the debt burden does not become too heavy, the sale of bonds usually means more after-tax profits for the stockholders. Further, with seemingly unending inflation, debts can be paid off at a future date with cheaper dollars.

But debt becomes addictive. At a time of continuing inflation, with the economy slowing down and effective demand tapering off, further debt expansion becomes increasingly important, e.g., to finance the growth of consumer instalment buying and to keep the fires of speculation burning in the stock, commodities, and real-estate markets. And as difficulties arise from carrying a mounting debt load, businesses turn to still more borrowing to help repay their old debts and to meet interest charges.*

It is this growing dependence on debt that also explains in large measure the greater use of short-term borrowing to finance business operations. Concerned about the disproportionate ratio of debt to equity capital and faced with a secular rise in interest rates, businesses have turned more and more to short-term borrowing. This, they hoped, would tide them over. Business would keep on booming, profits would continue strong, so why get locked into high-interest, long-term bonds and mortgages? But reliance on short-term borrowing didn't work either, as can be seen from the data in Tables 3 and 4 (pages 100 and 102 respectively).

Table 3 depicts one aspect of the accelerating growth of

---

* On the importance of debt expansion in recent years, see: "The Long-Run Decline in Liquidity," *Monthly Review*, September 1970, "Keynesian Chickens Come Home to Roost," pp. 21-32 above, and "Banks: Skating on Thin Ice," pp. 33-53 above.

TABLE 4
Outstanding Short-term Debt
Nonfinancial Corporations

	(1)	(2)	(3)	(4)	(5)
				Outstanding Short-term Debt as a Percent of	
	Total Outstanding Short-term Debt[a]	*Annual Gross Corporate Product*	*Internal Funds Generated Each Year*[b]	*Gross Corporate Product*	*Internal Funds*
	Billions of $				
1950	20.4	151.7	22.4	13.4	91.1
1955	29.3	216.3	29.9	13.5	98.0
1960	45.3	273.1	33.3	16.6	136.0
1965	71.2	374.6	55.2	19.0	129.0
1970	128.9	516.1	63.7	25.0	202.4
1974	220.9	731.1	107.0	30.2	206.4

(a) Includes the same items as given in Note (b) to Table 3.

(b) Undistributed after-tax profits (adjusted for changes in the value of inventories) and depreciation allowances.

Source: Outstanding short-term debt—same as Table 3. Gross corporate product and internal funds—*Survey of Current Business,* various issues. The internal-funds data are called "Cash flow, net of dividends" in the gross national product accounts published in the *Survey of Current Business.*

short-term debt in the financing of corporate business. Short-term debt is always an important contributor to corporate finance. The typical practice is to borrow for short periods to cover the time interval between the purchase and processing of raw materials and the sale of the final products. Materials suppliers and wages have to be paid long before the income from the sale of finished goods is realized. Bank loans are commonly used to finance the fluctuating needs for such working capital, with loans expanding in the upward phase of the cycle and declining in the downward phase. This pattern holds for the period since the Second World War, except that something new is added in the 1960s. Up until then repayment of bank loans (and other forms of short-term credit) in recession years was either equal to or greater than new loans, so that the *net* short-term loans to corporations were negative in 1948, 1949, 1953, and 1954, and zero in 1958. Thus the fact that short-term loans represent 21.6 percent of external financing in 1950-1954 and 26.5 percent in 1955-1959, as can be seen in Table 3, is the result of averaging good and bad years: fairly high percentages in prosperous times offset by either negative or zero net loans in declining periods.

With the 1960s a new financial fashion shows up. Increasingly, short-term borrowing becomes a much greater proportion of external financing than in the preceding years, and no longer are there any years when net loans are brought down to zero or below. And that is why the percentages shown in the fourth column of Table 3 rise to heights far above those for the 1950s. (The decline in the *percentage* of short-term debt from 1965-1969 to 1970-1974 does not reflect any cessation in the vigorous expansion of short-term debt. It merely means that in the latter period the increase in money obtained from the stock market was greater than the rise in long- and short-term debt, due to a spurt in the flotation of stock issues in 1971 and 1972.)

The upshot of the greater reliance on short-term debt and the relevance of this development to the financial health of corporations can be examined in Table 4. The growth in outstanding short-term debt was somewhat restrained in the late 1940s and the 1950s because, as was pointed out above, there were years when net new debt was either zero or negative. But with this no longer being the case in the 1960s and thus far in the 1970s, the total amount of outstanding short-term debt has exploded.

The nub of the problem is that debts have to be repaid, and short-term debts can be called in the short run. Now as long as corporations borrowed from banks and other money-market sources to meet normal needs for working capital, prospective repayments did not need to create anxiety. However, as can be inferred from the fourth column of Table 4, short-term borrowing began to be used for much more than tiding firms over during the processing and selling stages. The short-term debt as a percent of gross corporate product skyrocketed from the 13 to 14 percent typical of the 1950s to over 30 percent in 1974. This no doubt means that more and more short-term debt was being used either for investment in fixed capital (an investment that pays off only in the longer run) or to extend credit to a firm's customers—a practice that merely builds the debt pyramid and therefore makes the whole credit network increasingly vulnerable to collapse.

The business and banking community, however, counts on a safety cushion: the surplus cash flow generated in the course of corporate activities. This means undistributed profits and depreciation allowances, which are shown in the column of Table 4 headed "Internal Funds Generated Each Year." These are the monies a company expects to use for replacing worn-out equipment, buying machines that will save on labor, expanding capacity, creating a sinking fund for repayment of long-term bonds, and, in an emergency, settling accounts with the lenders of the short-term funds. But here again potential trouble is quite apparent. Look at the last column of Table 4. There we can see that in the 1950s the internal funds generated from year to year were roughly sufficient to cover the accumulated outstanding short-term debt. Now notice how drastically the situation begins to change, especially in the early 1970s when short-term debt was more than twice as large as the internal funds generated annually.

Is there any wonder that the business community begins to cry alarm about a capital shortage just when inventories are huge and a large part of available plant and equipment is lying idle? For what they mean by capital shortage is a deficiency in *money capital.* What is the money capital needed for? To save the corporations from the mess they have got themselves into. And how can one generate more funds to meet the needs of the corporations? Why, raising profits of course.

A further aspect of the present corporate financial picture deserves attention: the growing burden of interest charges (Table 5, p. 106). The first column of this table presents actual net interest paid by nonfinancial corporations. But not all this is a cost to the corporations, since interest is tax-deductible. In column (2) we have therefore adjusted for the tax saving to show the actual cost of interest payments. This more realistic interest cost is then added to after-tax profits to show the total amount of interest plus profits, which is also an approximate measure of the corporation's return on its capital.*

What immediately hits the eye in Table 5 is the enormous increase of interest costs in the last 25 years, both absolutely and as a percentage of interest plus profits. As can be seen from column (5), interest costs rose from 2.3 percent in 1950 to 20.4 in 1975. This means that corporations could retain 97.7 percent of their return on capital in 1950 for their own use (dividends, debt repayment, and capital accumulation), but only 79.6 percent in 1975. The other side of the coin is that a larger share of the nonfinancial corporations' return on capital is siphoned off into the financial sector. For the former this is naturally perceived as a further manifestation of capital shortage.

One other point needs to be added in this connection. The figures in Table 5 are for all nonfinancial corporations. But within this category there are wide variations: some corporations are in much better shape than others. Some can meet their debt repayment schedules with an ample margin left over for capital accumulation, while others are in trouble and many (including even some very big ones like W. T. Grant) have already gone over the brink into bankruptcy. These troubled corporations are more than isolated cases; they are weak links in a chain, and the more that break the greater is the danger to the chain as a whole.

As already suggested, the only solution the corporations can see to their capital problems—which really means their liquidity problems—is a substantial increase in profit rates. The thirst for higher profits is obviously always present in capitalist enterprise, but for firms tottering on the brink of bankruptcy or a takeover

---

* But note that this is *not* a measure of the total surplus value in the Marxian sense which is realized in the corporation. That total would include a large part of executives' salaries, net rent payments by the corporation, most of sales costs (including bribes to actual or prospective customers), and profits hidden under the rubric of depreciation allowances. Some idea of the magnitude of the last item can be gained from the fact that in the depressed year of 1975, while after-tax corporate profits, as shown in Table 5, went down by under one billion dollars, depreciation allowances increased by $11.2 billion from $78.3 billion in 1974 to $89.5 billion in 1975. (See *Economic Report of the President*, 1976, p. 180.)

TABLE 5
Interest and Profits
Nonfinancial Corporations

	(1) Net Interest Paid	(2) Cost of Interest Payments[a]	(3) After-tax Profits	(4) Interest Cost plus Profits (2) + (3)	(5) Interest Cost as a Percent of Interest plus Profits (2) ÷ (4)
	Billions of $				
1950	0.9	0.5	21.6	22.1	2.3
1955	1.6	0.8	21.8	22.6	3.5
1960	3.0	1.5	20.3	21.8	6.9
1965	5.9	3.4	37.2	40.6	8.4
1970	15.0	7.6	27.9	35.5	21.4
1974	22.9	13.4	61.1	74.5	18.0
1975[b]	25.0	15.5	60.4	75.9	20.4

(a) Calculated on the basis of the relation between before and after tax profits of corporations in each year, as given in the gross national product accounts.

(b) Preliminary data.

Source: *Survey of Current Business,* various issues, except for preliminary estimate of 1975 profits which is taken from *Economic Report of the President* (Washington, D.C.: Superintendent of Documents, 1976). The net interest payment for 1975 is an estimate based on available data for the first three quarters of the year.

by a stronger corporation the need for more profits becomes a matter of life or death. Even though many of the large corporations are in no such immediate danger, their financial condition is nevertheless drifting in the same direction, and will no doubt continue to do so in view of the stagnation of the overall economy and the unlikelihood of a vigorous new boom in the visible future. So they too have a special sense of urgency these days about boosting profits.

The question, then, is how can corporate profits be increased. One way of course is to increase sales with profit rates remaining stable. But in a period like the present when sales decline or are sluggish on the upside, only higher profit *rates* can be relied on. To the capitalist class this can only mean a mix of the following: holding down workers' wages, still more intense exploitation of labor at the workplace, reduction of corporation taxes, direct or indirect government subsidies, and a free rein to raise prices.

The open avowal of such goals by capitalists and their spokespeople would, however, be impolitic and counterproductive, so what they do is seek to generate a more receptive atmosphere among the mass of workers and consumers, stressing their supposed solicitude for social needs. There isn't enough capital, they clamor, to get all the energy we need, to clean our air and water, and to raise labor productivity so that more can be sold at home and abroad, and hence more jobs can be created. They say "capital shortage," but what they mean is "profit shortage" and/or insufficient government subsidies to underwrite risky investments and to pay for pollution control. At the same time, to the extent that they convince people that there is indeed a capital shortage, this becomes an argument to reduce expenditures on public housing, health, and other urgent mass needs. After all, since more capital is supposed to be required and since there are limits to the supply, there must be a contraction somewhere in the economy.

One thing is sure, however: this is not meant to be an argument for the elimination of the huge sums of money capital regularly drained off into the financial superstructure. A sense of the magnitude of one such drain—into stock-market speculation—can be obtained from the data in Table 6.

TABLE 6

New Issues and Total Sales of Stock

	Estimated Proceeds from New Stock Issues	*Total Sales of Stocks on Registered Exchanges*
	Billions of $	
1965	2.2	89.2
1970	8.6	130.5
1971	13.0	185.0
1972	13.1	204.0
1973	11.0	177.9
1974	6.3	118.3
1975*	10.9	165.5

* Estimated by extending the averages for the first eight months of 1975 in the case of total sales and seven months in the case of new issues.
Source: *Survey of Current Business,* various issues.

As can be seen, the new capital raised through the stock markets absorbs only an insignificant proportion of the money operating in these markets. At most, as in 1971, the proceeds of new issues accounted for only seven percent of total sales. It is true, of course, that total sales do not provide an accurate measure of the funds tied up in stock speculation, since a given sum of money can effect multiple sales in the course of a year. Nevertheless, it is clear that many billions of dollars are devoted entirely to stock speculation and have nothing to do with the financing or expansion of production.*

The stock market represents only one area into which money capital is diverted. In addition, there is the money capital float in other forms of speculation: various commodity futures markets, foreign exchange futures, puts and calls for common stocks, and—last but not least—real estate. All of these activities, as it happens, are supported and even stimulated by benevolent tax laws. Gains made from transactions that stretch out more than six months are taxed at greatly reduced rates. In real estate an entire financial apparatus has evolved that creates huge tax benefits for the wealthy and at the same time fosters speculation and inflation in land prices and construction costs.

It might be supposed that if there were really a serious capital shortage of the kind we are continually being warned about, the Cassandras would propose basic changes in the tax laws and other measures to deflate the bloated speculative markets. But one does not toy with sacred institutions. Instead, an attack is leveled at government borrowing in the money market. And the way to weaken this presumed pressure on the supply of capital is to cut down on social services at all levels of government: eliminate or reduce services in hospitals, schools, mental institutions, publicly assisted housing, etc. The raid on social services has already begun and, with New York City's financial crisis serving as a scarecrow, is especially stark and demoralizing at state and local levels.

Another ingredient of the package of remedies advanced to cure the presumed capital shortage is a further reduction in corporation taxes. This is shamelessly advocated in the face of the

* It should be noted too that by no means all the money raised through new issues is used for real capital needs, such as plant and equipment. Much of it is typically used for financial purposes, e.g., to pay off outstanding debts or to finance the buying out of other companies.

fact that the contribution of corporate income taxes to federal revenues has for some time been shrinking. For the data on this, see Table 7. The proportion of federal revenue originating in corporation income taxes declined from 23.2 percent in 1960 to 14.5 percent in 1975. This resulted from several developments: on the one hand the relative increase in social security taxes, and on the other hand the direct lowering of corporate tax rates, as well as concessions made to corporations via more liberal tax-deductible depreciation allowances and the investment tax credit. Clearly, any further reduction in corporate taxation can only be compensated by an increase either in individual income-tax rates or in various types of sales taxes.

TABLE 7

Contribution of Corporation Income Taxes

Fiscal Year	*Corporation Income Taxes as a Percent of Total Federal Budget Receipts*
1960	23.2
1965	21.8
1970	16.9
1975	14.5

Source: Data for 1960, 1965, and 1970 from *Statistical Abstract of the United States, 1973* (Washington, D.C.: Superintendent of Documents, 1973). Data for 1975 from *Economic Report of the President* (Washington, D.C.: Superintendent of Documents, 1976).

There is, to conclude, a nice and hardly unexpected consistency in the whole capital-shortage affair. First, figures are juggled about and dressed up in seemingly scientific guise. This is then associated with echoes of the energy-crisis scare and the popular pressure for improving and protecting the environment. From these two elements answers are derived that aim, by one means or another, to reduce consumption so that investment can be increased—in spite of the obvious fact that there is little reason for businesses to increase investment if effective demand does not increase substantially. Behind this rickety façade, one can detect the financial morass into which industry and the banks have sunk. The capital-shortage hysteria, in the final analysis, is but the latest ideological campaign to help put the house of monopoly capital in better order—at the expense of the people.

Creeping Stagnation

December 1977

Hopes ran high as the economy began to turn around in the last quarter of 1975. The rosy expectations of a vigorous recovery, however, did not last long. Although at first the economic advance seemed to resemble the strong upswings of the cycles of the past 25 years, beginning in the summer of 1976 it became apparent that the recovery was quickly losing momentum. Moreover, the slowdown and the persistence of high rates of unemployment were not confined to the United States but characterized almost all advanced capitalist countries. This was bad enough. But what really began to worry the more serious business analysts was the weakness of capital investment, since sustained recovery depends on a healthy advance in capital accumulation. Thus *Business Week* wrote in its issue of September 13, 1976:

> The world's key economies may be exhibiting the outward signs of recovery, but the growth of capital spending—which should be rising with the recovery—is extraordinarily sluggish. Why spending is so slow is puzzling to economic policy-makers in the leading industrial countries.

This article originally appeared in the January 1977 issue of *Monthly Review*.

In fact, however, the lagging of capital investment and the general weakness of the recovery are far from puzzling events if they are viewed historically. The 1974-1975 recession sent forth clear signals that something new was in the wind, and the years that preceded the recession had already witnessed the emergence of unusually severe economic imbalances. Not all of these were particularly novel, but almost all of them had in the previous decade grown to such an extent that they stamped a new brand on the next phases of the cycle, the recession of 1974-1975 and the subsequent recovery of 1975-1976.

The latest downward swing of the business cycle was in a fundamental sense typical, since it was triggered by over-production relative to effective demand. Toward the end of the boom producers had begun to turn out more goods than could either be sold or prudently held in inventory. Stocks of unsold goods piled up in the warehouses and storerooms of manufacturers, wholesalers, and retailers. As a result, capitalists responded as they must: production was cut back and workers laid off.

But that was only part of the story this time, for the down-turn followed on the heels of a period of rapidly accelerating credit expansion and inflation, feverish speculation in real estate and other markets, a long decline in corporate liquidity, tottering of large banks, and, last but not least, international monetary crises. These interrelated developments had been intensifying since the late 1960s, and they left their mark on the 1974-1975 recession, producing not only the deepest decline since the end of the Second World War, but also the paradoxical continuation of an upward price spiral alongside mass unemployment and declining real consumer income.

Against this background, it should come as no surprise that the ensuing recovery would also display differences from earlier upturns. Indeed, the several phases of the current cycle —boom, recession, and recovery—are all of a piece, each one revealing in its own way that the long wave of expansion since the Great Depression of the 1930s has been receding. The crucial point is that the special factors which kept capital accumulation relatively strong during the 1950s and 1960s have been losing strength or actually disappearing. And because of this the capitalist world has been tending toward stagnation, an economic condition in which deep recessions and weak recoveries are to be expected.*

The distinctive features of this new stage of stagnation become strikingly apparent when the extraordinary amount of government financial stimulus involved in the most recent turnaround from recession to recovery is contrasted with the experience of the recessions of the 1950s and 1960s. As is well known, bourgeois economists and government policy-makers pin their hopes on federal budget deficits to start the ball rolling when the economy falters, expecting in this way to fill a growing gap between demand and production capacity. The reasoning is quite simple. The effect of a balanced budget on the economy, it is held, is usually neutral: the lowering of demand by individuals and businesses due to tax payments is offset by an equal demand created by government spending.** But when the government spends more than it takes in, total demand for goods and services increases, and, assuming there is sufficient idle capacity and unemployment, the economy is stimulated to produce more and create more jobs. (A deficit develops automatically during recessions as long as government spending remains level, since tax collections decline along with reduced employment and income; an increase in government spending under these circumstances will naturally enlarge the deficit.)

Now let us look at what has been happening in this area. Table 1 (page 114) presents information for recession years since the Second World War, along with annual data since 1971. What cries out for attention in the first column of this table is the exceptionally large $71.2 billion federal deficit in 1975 as compared with deficits of previous recessions. Before we attempt to interpret this enormous difference, however, we must ask whether

---

* A fuller discussion of this point is presented in "The Economic Crisis in Historical Perspective," Parts I and II, pp. 21-32 and 33-53 above.

** This is of course an oversimplification, since government spending may have a greater or smaller impact on the rest of the economy than the purchases which individuals and businesses would have made if taxes had been lower.

TABLE I

	Federal Government Deficit		*Gross National Product (GNP) of Private Economy*	*Deficit as % of GNP (Column 2 ÷ column 3 x 100)*
	Billions of Current $	*Billions of Constant $*	*Billions of Constant $*	
	(1)	(2)	(3)	(4)
1949	2.6	6.2	426.7	1.5
1953	7.1	14.1	534.9	2.6
1958	10.3	17.7	586.1	3.0
1967	13.2	18.2	874.6	2.1
1971	22.0	23.8	964.3	2.5
1972	17.3	17.3	1,026.7	1.7
1973	6.9	6.5	1,087.0	0.6
1974	11.7	10.0	1,065.5	0.9
1975	71.2	54.8	1,042.6	5.3
1976 (1st half)	59.0	42.9	1,101.6	3.9

Source: Data from *Survey of Current Business* (January, September, and October 1976). The data in column 1 are not the official federal budget figures, but are adjusted by the Commerce Department for comparability with the gross national product accounts. Column 2 was calculated using the implicit price index for federal government purchases of goods and services, with 1972=100. Column 3 represents the gross domestic national product minus federal, state, and local government components. Data for the first half of 1976 are at an annual rate.

it is simply the consequence of (1) inflation or (2) the increasing size of the economy as a whole. To answer the first question, column 2 provides the deficit statistics adjusted for price changes. Here we see that even in constant dollars the 1975 deficit was more than three times as high as the largest deficit in the 1950s and 1960s, and almost two and a half times the 1971 deficit. Note also that even as the economy recovered —in the first half of 1976—the deficit remained considerably higher than in any previous postwar year except 1975.* And to answer the second question, column 4 compares the deficits of each year with the gross national product of the private economy in the same years, showing that the *relative* size of the deficit in 1975 is 80 percent above the highest previous per-

* To simplify the presentation, not all the high-deficit years are shown in Table 1. None of the excluded years, however, contradicts this statement. Thus there were only two other years when the deficits, in constant dollars, reached above $10 billion: 1954—$11.9 billion, and 1970—$14 billion.

centage (5.3 percent in 1975 compared to 3 percent in 1958). Moreover, even in 1976, a recovery year, the government ran a deficit that relative to private gross national product was significantly greater than in the recession year of 1958.

TABLE 2

	Federal Government Deficit	*Gross Private Investment*	*Deficit as % of Private Investment (Column 1 ÷ column 2 x 100)*
	In billions of current $		
	(1)	(2)	(3)
1949	2.6	35.3	7.4
1953	7.1	53.3	13.3
1958	10.3	61.9	16.6
1967	13.2	120.8	10.9
1971	22.0	160.0	13.8
1972	17.3	188.3	9.2
1973	6.9	220.5	3.1
1974	11.7	215.0	5.4
1975	71.2	183.7	38.8
1976 (1st half)	59.0	234.4	25.2

Source: Same as Table 1.

Still more instructive are the figures in Table 2 showing the size of the deficit compared to gross private domestic investment. The three types of business investment included under this heading—inventory accumulation, residential construction, and plant and equipment (machinery, factories, power stations, etc.)—are the most important levers of the business cycle. They are the prime movers which pull the economy up and push it forward during prosperity periods and exert the major downward pressures during recessions and depressions. What is especially noteworthy, therefore, is that even in the 1950s, when the underlying expansionist forces in the private economy were still relatively strong, the government's supporting stimulus kept on increasing from recession to recession. Thus, in 1949 the deficit was only 7.4 percent of private investment, rising to 13.3 percent in 1953 and 16.6 percent in 1958. This by itself suggests that the growth elements in the private economy were already showing signs of weakening toward the end of the 1950s.

Signs of the approaching exhaustion of the long postwar

wave of expansion cropped up more frequently beginning in the 1960s. But it is also in this period that there was a persistent tendency in Washington to raise spending levels. By 1974 federal government purchases of goods and services (in constant dollars) were almost 50 percent above 1960. Yet despite the increasing role of government, and the spur provided by the war in Vietnam and an enormous growth of credit, the normal capitalist tendency toward stagnation became increasingly powerful, with recession declines in gross capital investment—the area where the stagnation forces are lodged—steadily rising: in constant dollars, the drop in the 1953-1954 recession was 12 percent, in 1957-1958 it was 19 percent, finally reaching as much as 40 percent between the fourth quarter of 1973 and the second quarter of 1975.

These stagnationist trends in government deficits and private investment have resulted in a startling relative increase in the size (and importance) of the deficit component—from an average of less than 8 percent of private investment in the years 1971-1974 to a startling 39 percent in the recession year 1975, falling only to 25 percent in the recovery of the first half of 1976. And even with this enormous increase in the government stimulus—provided, ironically, by a fiscally conservative Republican administration—there has been no significant reduction in unemployment, which by official count has remained well above 7 percent of the labor force through recession and recovery (and which at the moment of writing in December 1976 has risen above 8 percent for the first time in a year).*

Let us now look more closely at the three major components of private investment. In the short run the decisive propellent of the cycle is business investment in inventories. When consumer demand is on the upswing, factory production expands not only to meet rising sales but also to fill up the pipelines of raw materials, components, and wholesale and retail stocks of finished goods. In addition, businessmen expand inventories in anticipation of still further growth in consumer

---

* For background on the growth and persistence of unemployment, see "Capitalism and Unemployment," pp. 77-90 above.

demand. Capitalism, however, puts narrow limits on the growth of consumer incomes, and the market soon proves that the pace of production is excessive. Capitalists then seek to protect their profits and reduce their risks by cutting back on production and laying off workers. This, normally occurring in a broad spectrum of industries at about the same time, triggers a general decline which in turn becomes self-reinforcing. Inventories which until recently had seemed too small now appear to be excessive. They are sold off and not replaced, resulting in a still further cutback in production. (Statistically, this is reflected in a *negative* rate of inventory investment.) But this downward movement is also self-limiting. Provided there are no additional factors depressing demand, the cycle begins over again: production expands first to satisfy existing markets, then to rebuild inventories; employment and income rise; sales increase; and the business world is back on the road to overproduction.

What has just been described is generally known as the "inventory cycle," and it operates in good times and bad—during the 1930s as well as during the 1950s, 60s, and 70s. But it tells us nothing about the forces which determine whether the economy is buoyant or stagnant, nor more particularly about the probability of its being able to provide jobs for a growing labor force. To understand these crucially important matters, we need to examine some more basic aspects of capitalist society and its mode of operation.

Capitalists' total receipts from sales can be divided into three parts: the wage bill which is spent by workers on consumer goods; depreciation intended for the replacement of worn-out or obsolete machinery (and other capital goods); and "surplus" to be distributed to members of the capitalist class and their lieutenants in the form of profits, interest, rent, and (often enormous) salaries. The surplus is much more than its recipients can or want to spend on consumer goods, so the remainder (plus what is set aside as depreciation) must be invested if the whole economy is to keep running smoothly. And the kind of investment which is required here is not in the inherently unstable field of inventories but rather in the other two categories of private investment, residential construction and plant and equipment, which are the essential growth elements in a capitalist economy. Without the full use of the surplus for investment of this kind, stagnation becomes the order of the day: built-up capacity cannot be fully utilized on a profitable basis; unemployment grows since there are no jobs for new entrants to the labor market and those displaced by advancing technology; slumps tend to be more severe and recoveries to be sluggish.

TABLE 3

Business Investment

(Seasonally adjusted totals at annual rates, in billions of 1972 dollars)

	Change in Business Inventories	*Residential Construction*	*Non-residential Plant and Equipment*
1974			
I	+12.4	49.1	134.5
II	+ 6.8	47.1	129.9
III	+ 4.2	44.1	125.0
IV	+ 7.6	38.5	120.8
1975			
I	-20.5	35.4	114.4
II	-21.2	36.8	110.6
III	- 1.0	39.6	110.1
IV	- 5.5	41.9	110.5
1976			
I	+10.4	44.1	112.6
II	+11.1	45.7	114.9
III	+ 9.9	46.9	117.0

Source: Same as Table 1.

Now it is weakness in precisely these decisive investment fields that characterizes the present economic situation. As far as the inventory cycle is concerned, it has been going through its paces as expected (Table 3). Note that column 1 of Table 3 depicts *changes* in inventory holdings from quarter to quarter, not total investment as in the other two columns. A minus sign in column 1 means that a decline in inventory has taken place, while a plus indicates additions. As is evident from Table 3, the inventory pipeline was still being filled up during 1974. In 1975, on the other hand, production was curtailed and inventories were sold off in each quarter of that year. A pick-up in business in 1976, in turn, was pushed further along by a fairly quick rebuilding of stocks. But while the general contours of this cyclical behavior resemble that of preceding recessions, there was a major difference this time in that the recovery was helped along by unusual stimulation from both government and business. First, there was the extraordinary spur provided by the tax cuts and other special government measures in early 1975: steps that produced (as seen in Table 4, page 112) a deficit in the second quarter which amounted at an annual rate to almost $100 billion. Even this was not enough to get rid of the enormous backlog of cars in the hands of dealers and to pave the way for a recovery in auto production. In this situation, auto manufacturers, banks, and finance companies went all out by stretching credit to unheard-of limits, ignoring entirely the impact these practices might have in depressing auto markets in future years. Read, for example, how the *Wall Street Journal* described this development:

> In a sharp departure from auto financing practices of the past two decades, you can buy a new car at a growing number of places these days without putting so much as a penny down. Becoming almost as common are terms requiring less than 10 percent down. In both cases, monthly payments often are comfortably below $100.
>
> But there's one catch: those low payments are made possible only by stretching out the length of the loan, from a couple of years in the good old days, to four—and sometimes even five—years now. . . . From the mid-1950s until a few years ago, even the most creditworthy auto buyers generally were limited to financing no more than 80 percent of a car's retail price and to terms no longer than 36 months. As recently as September 1974, government figures show, only about 10 percent of new-car loans by major finance companies were for longer than 36 months. But just a year later, fully one quarter of the new-car loans by these lenders were exceeding this traditional maximum. (January 8, 1976)

Yet despite these props to retail sales and the consequent fairly rapid turnaround in the inventory cycle, the other types of business investment have been unable to get back to previous peaks, let alone surpass them as would be necessary for this type of business investment to have a significant impact on unemployment.

In the case of residential construction, it should be recognized that this industry had been in a critical condition for some time before the recent recession. The postwar peak in home-building was reached in 1972, when $62 billion were invested in this field. Since then activity dropped 43 percent to a low point of $35.4 billion in the first quarter of 1975. Ironically, this precipitous drop, starting in the midst of a cyclical upswing, was itself triggered by the prosperity it helped to create. The latter, sustained by a wave of credit expansion, produced such a tightness in the availability of mortgage money and such high interest rates that the housing market was strangled. And since the onset of the recession was accompanied by a loosening of mortgage money and a drop in interest rates, the construction industry began to turn around at an early stage in the recession. Helping along was the backlog in demand for housing that accumulated during the years of sharply declining construction. Yet despite the more favorable financial conditions and the potential demand, the recovery was slow. By the third quarter of 1976, construction activity was still only about 75 percent of the former high.

Aware of the infirmities of the home-building field and the limitations of an upswing stemming mainly from the inventory factor, bourgeois economists and government policy-makers have been pinning their hopes for a durable recovery on investment in additional productive capacity—a development that it was hoped would be strong enough to allay some of the more serious social problems (mass unemployment, the financial crisis of the cities, etc.) besetting the country. So far, however, the recovery of investment for replacement, modernization, and capacity expansion has been far from encouraging, as noted in the quotation from *Business Week* on page one above. Instead of fueling the recovery by energetic growth programs, the business community has been dragging its feet. As can be seen from the third column of Table 3, investment in plant and equipment advanced barely 6 percent in a full year of recovery (from the third quarter of 1975 to the third quarter of 1976); even at that it was still 13 percent below the preceding peak reached in the first quarter of 1974.

This loss of vitality is, in reality, far from a new development. The special underlying forces that sustained the long postwar expansion have been petering out for at least a decade now. This process, however, has been masked by extremes of speculation and credit creation that, along with a resultant speed-up in inflation, helped push up production to beyond limits which would normally have been set by available consumer incomes. In the nature of the case, such artificial stimulation could be no more than a temporary palliative. Sooner or later the credit bubble bursts and leads to serious business contractions and failures.* Considering the shaky foundations of the most recent economic expansions, it is little wonder that business firms are exceptionally cautious in their investment policies.**

Despite much interested propaganda to the contrary, one thing is eminently clear: the slowness of the recovery of investment in plant and equipment has not been due to any shortage of money. For one of the outstanding features of the present cycle has been a substantial improvement in corporate finances in the midst of, and in spite of, the recession. In this respect, Table 4 tells an interesting and instructive story. The first column shows the quarterly growth of the federal deficit. The second column presents the corporate surplus in each of the

---

* For analysis of the role of credit expansion and its limits, see "Keynesian Chickens Come Home to Roost," pp. 21-32 above, "Banks: Skating on Thin Ice," pp. 33-53 above, and "Capital Shortage: Fact and Fancy," pp. 91-108 above.

** There are also fundamental historical forces at work here which cannot be dealt with in a brief analysis. Of particular relevance is the slowdown in the suburbanization of the population with a consequent reduction or cessation in the demand for a great variety of goods and services (highways, streets, utilities, schools, hospitals, stores, etc.). The fact that similar or comparable goods and services are urgently *needed* in decaying city centers is unfortunately entirely unrelated to the question of profitable investment opportunities. This whole issue of the historical climate for private investment has been almost totally ignored by the economic pundits and forecasters. Some businessmen have been more perceptive: see, e.g., the excellent piece, "The Capital Shortage—A False Alarm," by Robert S. Wall, a New York investment counsellor, in the Sunday financial section of the *New York Times* (November 7, 1976).

same quarters (pre-tax profits plus depreciation reserves).* (The quarterly data are expressed in annual rates for ease in comparison with annual totals.) Two aspects of the corporate

TABLE 4

	Federal Government Deficit	*Corporate Surplus (Profits before taxes plus depreciation reserves)*
	Billions of $, quarterly data at annual rates, seasonally adjusted	
1974		
I	5.3	162.8
II	7.9	165.6
III	8.0	162.7
IV	25.5	158.1
1975		
I	49.8	158.5
II	99.9	179.5
III	66.0	201.9
IV	69.4	205.6
1976		
I	63.8	216.2
II	54.1	221.2

Source: Same as Table 1.

surplus series are particularly striking. Note first that a decline in the surplus took place only in the earliest stage of the recession, and even then was minimal: 3 percent between the first and fourth quarters of 1974. After that, during the severest postwar recession, the corporate surplus kept on rising—jumping 30 percent between the low point in the last quarter of 1974 and the last quarter of 1975, and continuing to move ahead into 1976. In effect, what has been happening is that the federal deficit ended up finally in the coffers of the corporations: the increase in the deficit between the fourth quarters of 1974 and 1975 amounted to almost $44 billion (from $25.5

* These data are based on new revisions made by the Commerce Department in the gross national product and national income accounts. At the time of writing, comparable data on corporate income taxes are not yet available. A more accurate picture of corporate funds available for investment would of course need an adjustment for corporate tax obligations. We believe, however, that the unadjusted figures shown in Table 4 are significant in showing the main trend.

to $69.4 billion), while the corporate surplus rose by almost $48 billion (from $158.1 to $205.6 billion). This very close coincidence is of course in part a statistical fluke. But behind it lies a significant aspect of the present U.S. economy, as well described by Professor V Lewis Bassie:

> There is an increasingly marked tendency for gross corporate saving to recover strongly as the federal deficit mounts. Deficits appear to be largely and ever more quickly absorbed into corporate surpluses. Part of this is intended; it comes from tax cuts and higher investment allowances. Even more it derives from the price system, which acts as a transfer system to benefit those whose power to raise prices is unrestricted. This helps to explain why inflation and recession go together.*

If these swollen funds are not fueling a substantial rise in investment, what are they being used for? The answer to this question summarizes, in a sense, the entire business scene in a period of stagnation. Industrial firms and financial institutions have been growing by blowing up the debt balloon, stretching it almost to the bursting point. The slowdown during the recession and the growth in the corporate surplus have enabled the larger corporations to get their financial affairs in better order: bank loans have been repaid, short-term debt converted into long-term debt, and cash reserves set aside for working capital. This has resulted in a definite improvement in corporate liquidity.**

This is naturally a comfort and a solace to the corporations and their functionaries, stockholders, and dependents. But in a climate of creeping stagnation it is hardly a message of cheer to the unemployed, the vast majority of workers whose real incomes have been contracting for several years now, the

---

* V. Lewis Bassie, "Fiscal Policy Without Controls," *Illinois Business Review,* December 1975. Bassie, who was the first one to make the comparison between corporate surplus and the deficit, discusses the issue in a further article "Cyclical Effects of Deficit Spending," in the same journal, February 1976.

** The counterpart of course has been a huge increase in the federal debt—from $486 billion on July 1, 1974, to $648 billion on July 1, 1976, i.e., an increase of one third in only two years. What has been happening on an unprecedented scale, in other words, is a shift of part of the debt burden from the corporate (private) sector to the government (public) sector.

crisis-ridden cities and their harried officials, the millions of others who (because of old age, bad health, or insecure jobs) live on the brink of disaster in this richest of all countries. Capital accumulation is the key to the performance of every capitalist economy, and this depends not on the availability of money or credit but on the existence of profitable opportunities to invest.

In the past, new waves of such profitable opportunities appeared from time to time, and it certainly cannot be precluded that this will happen again. As the saying goes, hope springs eternal. But it might make more sense to begin seriously to think about replacing a system which depends entirely on the profits of the rich by one which does away with profits altogether and operates solely with a view to meeting the real needs of ordinary people. It is not a new idea, but the crazy situation in which we now find ourselves suggests that maybe it is an idea whose time has come.

Keynesianism: Illusions and Delusions

April 1977

Facts and history notwithstanding, the ideology of our times continues to be permeated by the belief that governments of capitalist societies have the knowledge and ability to eliminate economic fluctuations and achieve permanent full employment. The recent course of events has begun to introduce some tremors of doubt, but the resulting sprouts of skepticism have still not shaken economists, government officials, businessmen, trade-union leaders, and the public at large out of their ultimate trust in the magical powers of government economic intervention. An interesting example of a fairly typical confrontation of fact with faith is contained in a recent report prepared by a Yale economics professor for the Joint Congressional Economic Committee, which starts with the following striking summation of U.S. economic performance since the end of the Second World War:

> *In the last three decades, the United States economy has not achieved full employment except under the pressure of war demand; recoveries abort before full employment can be achieved, and continuous growth is not sustainable.* The record shows that since World War II there have been 10 years of recession, 12 years of recovery, and 7 years under the influence of wartime pressures.

This article originally appeared in the April 1977 issue of *Monthly Review*.

Of the 6 recovery periods, 4 aborted into recessions before full employment was reached, and the other two merged into the Korean and Vietnam wars. Recoveries are so short-lived that a new recession is always just around the corner. Thus, in the short run, growth is frustrated in recovery and eroded by recession, and consequently, long-term economic growth is reduced to a level considerably below its potential.*

Having fired this salvo, and adding to it other interesting factual observations, what does the author then conclude? A new and improved government medicine should be prescribed—as if in previous decades all that had been lacking to provide full employment was the right mixture of formulas.

This is of course symptomatic of a condition which has characterized bourgeois economics practically from the beginning. Each economist or school of economics has sought to overcome the contradictions of capitalism by ignoring their roots in the system itself. Instead, one or another set of reforms has been advocated in the hope that the recommended changes would make an irrational system behave in a more efficient and pleasant fashion. Traditional "economic science" insisted that a deficiency in demand—or, in other words, a general overproduction of goods and services—was just impossible. This was because capitalist markets provided a remarkable adjustment mechanism, and because savings—the amount of income not used to buy consumer goods—would all be spent by capitalists for investment. Maladjustments in some parts of the economy would of course always occur, but these distortions would induce sufficient changes in prices and profits to maintain total production and total consumption in balance. Operating within such an optimistic framework, economists, government officials, and other propagators of the ruling ideology confronted depressions and the accompanying misery with equanimity. Crises were attributed either to acts of God or to human error. Mistakes made by officials of the government or of the central bank could be corrected and, hopefully, avoided in the

* Richard Ruggles, "Economic Growth in the Short Run: Its Behavior and Measurement," in Joint Economic Committee, Congress of the United States, *U.S. Economic Growth from 1976 to 1986: Prospects, Problems, and Patterns,* vol. 2, (Washington, D.C.: U.S. Government Printing Office, November 10, 1976), p. 1.

future. Meanwhile, patience and restraint were called for, since the market in its infinite wisdom would before long set things right again.

But this sort of faith in a self-regulating capitalist economy was hard to cling to in the midst of the Great Depression of the 1930s when disorder reigned in almost every area of domestic and international economic affairs, and social upheaval threatened the established order. The masses in the capitalist world were becoming increasingly aware that economic crises were not just chance occurrences, especially in view of the absence of depression and unemployment in the Soviet Union. But it wasn't only the unemployed—and the employed whose wages were cut supposedly to enable the market to assert its benevolence—who demanded change. Disaster-ridden farmers and small businessmen, and even many huge corporations threatened by bankruptcy, added to the pressure for drastic remedial action. In response, governments desperately experimented with measures designed to keep the ship of state afloat. But the academic economists, no matter how uncomfortable they may have felt about the gap between their theory and reality, had little to offer beyond a pious repetition of their traditional litany.

Under these circumstances, the revolt against the orthodox ideology initiated by the publication in 1936 of Keynes' *General Theory of Employment, Interest, and Money* quickly found a receptive audience. There were several reasons for the relative ease with which the new doctrines were absorbed: (1) They came from a most respectable source. Keynes himself was an outstanding, perhaps even the most eminent, theoretician of the economics establishment, and he was backed up by a strong nucleus of authoritative Cambridge University colleagues. (2) The revolutionary aspects of the new theory were palatable insofar as they were clearly intended to rescue a crumbling capitalism.* (3) A theoretical framework was provided to rationalize and systematize actions that governments were being forced to

* "Whilst, therefore, the enlargement of the functions of government involved in the task of adjusting to one another the propensity to consume and the inducement to invest, would seem to a nineteenth-century

undertake to cope with the current extraordinary depression. (Coincidentally, this also gave economists entry to the upper regions of the state.) And (4) enough leeway was provided to permit integration of the Keynesian heresy into the established school of economic thought—in fact, strengthening their role as apologists for the capitalist system.

At the heart of the Keynesian system is the recognition that "free" markets do not automatically create harmony between total production and total consumption—hardly a new idea, of course, to students of Marx. Depressions can therefore arise from the normal functioning of the capitalist economy. A state of general overproduction, which the classical economists banished from their realm of discourse, is not only possible but indeed likely from time to time. Keynes, however, did not talk about overproduction; he put his finger on the opposite side of the coin—a deficiency in effective demand. Without going into technical details, we can say that Keynes held that the business cycle begins to turn down because a portion of income saved, i.e., withheld from consumption, is not neatly counterbalanced by the willingness of capitalists to invest in new plant and equipment. In other words there is no necessary correspondence between the investment decisions of corporations and the amount of money kept off the market by the accumulation of profits plus the savings of the rich. Keynes then argued that intelligent and energetic government action was needed to remedy this defect in the market system. Either income should be redistributed so that there would be more buying of consumer goods by the poorer segments of the population, or the government should spend enough money to compensate for the lack of business investment activity.

This savings-and-investment theory has by now become the common currency of economic thinking among lay people as well as professionals. But it is little recognized that Keynes'

---

publicist or to a contemporary American financier to be a terrific encroachment on individualism, I defend it, on the contrary, both as the only practicable means of avoiding the destruction of existing economic forms in their entirety and as the condition of the successful functioning of individual initiative." John Maynard Keynes, *The General Theory of Employment, Interest, and Money* (London: Macmillan & Co., 1936), p. 380.

vision went far beyond simple government manipulation of a few economic variables. In the final chapter of his *General Theory,* entitled "Concluding Notes on the Social Philosophy Toward Which the General Theory Might Lead," he tackles what he sees to be the basic faults and diseases of capitalism. In addition to the problems associated with recurrent business cycles, he points to a general failure to provide full employment even in times of prosperity, "arbitrary and inequitable distribution of wealth and income," wars caused by the pressure of population and the competitive struggle for markets, and manipulation of foreign trade for the purpose of shifting domestic economic troubles onto the shoulders of other countries.

These ills, Keynes believed, could ultimately be overcome by gradual changes in some of the more important institutions of capitalism. Thus, he predicted, and considered necessary, a marked decline in the rate of profit and the eventual elimination of the part of surplus value that goes to pay interest. In effect what he saw was a need for the dissolution of finance capital, leaving only industrial capital to operate with a minimal profit rate. Along this line, he talked about "the euthanasia of the rentier, and, consequently, the euthanasia of the cumulative oppressive power of the capitalist to exploit the scarcity-value of capital." (p. 376) This development, together with effective inheritance and other tax policies would work toward the elimination of great differences in wealth and income—a basic change that would be needed not only for the sake of social justice but as a valuable aid in the achievement of permanent full employment. Ultimately, however, "a somewhat comprehensive socialization of investment will prove the *only* means of securing an approximation to full employment." (p. 378, emphasis added) What he meant by this was state determination, year by year, of the percent of total output going to investment, as well as of the rate of profit. If this were done effectively, then there would be no need, according to Keynes, for the abolition of capitalist ownership of the means of production. All that would be needed for the smooth functioning of the economy was government control over total investment and profits; individual capitalists could be relied upon to make the decisions about what and how much needs to be produced.

In short, the thrust of Keynes' thought was to rescue capitalism from the threat and necessity of socialism. For this purpose, he proposed reforms that eventually would, on the one hand, do away with the leisure and finance-capital classes, and, on the other hand, keep a tight rein on the remaining managerial and entrepreneurial capitalists. He certainly had no illusion that the simple manipulation of taxes, interest rates, and government spending would suffice to achieve and maintain full employment, and at the same time abolish poverty and eradicate the forces that lead to wars and international trade rivalries. His illusions were of an entirely different kind. He ignored, and in fact denied, the power exercised by the capitalist class to defend its ownership rights and its freedom to seek ever larger profits. Philosophically, he was an idealist pure and simple. Keynes himself put the case as strongly as anyone ever has: "The ideas of economists and political philosophers, both when they are right and when they are wrong, are more powerful than is commonly understood. Indeed the world is ruled by little else." (p. 383)

If ever an advanced thinker had reason to expect his ideas to influence, and even dominate, economic policy in the Western world, it was surely Keynes. Let us see, though, what happened in the next 40 years, during most of which Keynesian ideas were in the ascendant. An argument might be made that the application of these doctrines altered the *shape* of the recurrent business cycle. Business cycles, however, were far from eliminated. And what about the more basic changes that Keynes claimed were needed to stabilize and purify capitalist societies? Poverty has surely not been abolished, nor has there been significant decrease, if any, in the unequal distribution of wealth. Instead of the euthanasia of the rentier, we find a vigorous growth of banking, finance companies, and other moneylenders; while interest payments keep on taking an increasingly larger share of surplus value. Not peace, but a steady dose of war. Not great harmony among international trading partners, but the resurgence of trade rivalries—and no diminution in the exploitation of the Third World by the centers of imperialism. Despite the use of Keynesian palliatives, the leading capitalist nation has not been able to reach full employment except in time of war. And in those countries that have engaged in more advanced forms of government intervention—such as planning and operating state-owned enterprises—the result has been to strengthen and preserve monopoly-capitalist interests, not to clip their wings.

The fate of the Keynesian program is itself a fitting commentary on Keynes' belief that it is ideas rather than interests that rule the world. There can be no question that an idea, when its time has come, can have enormous influence. But social and political ideas do not merely have a life of their own: their power arises from the use made of them by people, and most particularly by social classes. When a set of ideas fits in with the interests of a given class, it may be directly absorbed as a guide to action. Ideas, on the other hand, that in part conform and in other respects conflict with the vested interests have another destiny: they are twisted and contorted into a shape that suits the class that adopts them. And this is exactly what happened to Keynes' grand vision of the need for a different kind of capitalism.

Since the time was ripe for a rejection of the obsolete optimism of earlier economists and for a more energetic involvement of governments in economic affairs, bourgeois economists were quick to welcome the new Keynesian doctrines. But this was done to serve their own purposes. They thus ignored not only Keynes' attempt at a diagnosis of the ills of capitalism, but even his illusions about capitalism's reforming itself to compete with socialism. Instead they chose to accept some of Keynes' technical innovations, which were soon integrated into the established orthodox economics—resulting in what has become known in the economics trade as the "neoclassical synthesis," aptly called by Joan Robinson "bastard Keynesianism."

The net result was an updated version of bourgeois economics; while continuing to wear the costume of objective science, it continued to perform its customary role as apologist for the capitalist system. The existing order was assumed to be durable and permanent, intrinsically harmonious, and destined to keep on expanding. Maladjustments would creep in from time to time, especially when savings exceeded investment. But then the Keynesian tool-kit was there to be put to work. After that, harmony and growth would return to normal. These theories were wrapped up in elaborate mathematical formulas, ostensibly demonstrating their scientific rigor. The practitioners of this magic science were now convinced that they had all the answers: they knew exactly how to regulate the economy and prevent depressions.

It did not take long for these enticing notions to become embedded in the ruling ideology, since they germinated and grew during the long wave of prosperity following the Second World War. In the absence of an understanding of the roots of this prosperity—in the stabilization of the imperialist world under U.S. hegemony, the rapid spread of new industries, the growth of militarism—credit was given to the new Keynesianism for the "successes" achieved by the advanced capitalist nations and for the nonrecurrence of a major depression.

Yet along with the growing enchantment with this new bag of tricks, some skepticism did begin to crop up. For basic to the notion that fluctuations in economic performance could be avoided was a confidence that potential declines in business could be pinpointed in advance and in sufficient time to take counteracting measures. But it wasn't long before reality began to intrude: despite the growing sophistication of forecasting techniques, no economist has uncovered the secret of reliable prediction. (This is not so surprising, considering the anarchy of capitalist production.) Most significant in this connection was the inability of forecasters, using the most advanced econometric models and computers, to anticipate even six months ahead the worst postwar recession of 1974-1975. If such a severe downturn could not be reliably predicted, what hope was there to take action to prevent the decline, even assuming the ability to do so?

Furthermore, despite the presumption that there exists a *science* of business-cycle control, there has never been general agreement on the best techniques to use. Each new crop of would-be economic advisers, using the same Keynesian tool-kit but confronted with a new set of political and economic conditions, has come up with different, and often conflicting, recommendations. This is hardly the sort of performance to support the claim about the existence of a reliable, scientific method of regulating the economy. Meanwhile capitalist reality has displayed more than recurrent business cycles—spiraling inflation together with a secular rise in the rate of unemployment, explosion of private and public debts, extreme financial difficulties (bordering on outright financial crises in 1966, 1970, and 1973-1974), the collapse of the international monetary system put in place after the Second World War.

The stark contrast between the standard Keynesian textbook theory and the developments in the real world has begun to stimulate a serious re-examination of the theory by some economists. One of the most interesting and penetrating of these new critiques is a recent book, *John Maynard Keynes,* by Hyman P. Minsky (New York: Columbia University Press, 1975). Minsky, professor of economics at Washington University in St. Louis, argues that the "bastard Keynesians" have oversimplified Keynes and have succeeded in producing a puerile theory that neither recognizes nor understands the innate instability of a capitalist economy. He attempts to re-interpret Keynes with a view to bringing out new analytical elements that he believes are implicit in *The General Theory.* Whether they are or are not implicit in Keynes is beside the point for our present purpose; what is of real interest is that Minsky introduces new and more realistic dimensions of economic analysis that go a long way toward exposing the illusory nature of the prevailing faith in a scientific way to control and regulate capitalism.*

The crucial missing element in the standard Keynesian theory, according to Minsky, is adequate "consideration of capitalist finance within a cyclical and speculative context." (p. 129) If one thinks only in terms of consumption and investment, the destabilizing consequences of the economy's dependence on debt and speculation are overlooked. The fact is that economic up-

---

* See especially "Keynesian Chickens Come Home to Roost," pp. 21-32, "Banks: Skating on Thin Ice," pp. 33-53, and "Creeping Stagnation," pp. 111-124, all above.

swings are not balanced affairs, with consumption and investment neatly coordinated in a rational pattern—nor can they be, even with the best-intentioned government intervention, so long as investment and production decisions are governed by profit expectations. As new profit opportunities loom on the horizon, the upward phase of the cycle is spurred and accelerated by an increase in borrowing; and the growing credit structure is supported by hope and faith that the boom will never end. Corporations raise the money they need to expand by selling bonds or borrowing from the banks. Consumer purchases are blown up by an inflation of retail, installment, and mortgage credit, encouraged and facilitated by the lending practices of banks and finance companies. The banks in turn sell off their conservative investment in government bonds in order to get hold of more money to lend to businesses, consumers, and speculators who ride on the coattails of the boom. As the demand for bank money increases, the banks in their drive for profits stretch their lending to the limit and even become borrowers themselves in order to carry on their money-lending activities.

In a very real sense, all elements entering the debt stretch-out are different forms of speculation. Consumers rely on their continuing to have jobs and sufficient income to meet interest charges and eventually pay off their debts. For the same reason, manufacturers count on an uninterrupted growth in sales and profits. The outright speculators buy commodities, real estate, and stocks on the assumption that the prices will just keep on rising. And, finally, the bankers themselves must hope for smooth sailing in the economy as a whole so that at some future time they will be able to pay back to depositors and lenders the money they have been playing with.

In reality, however, all such speculation is precariously based. Any slowdown in the economic advance can cause the financial structure to tremble. An excess accumulation of inventories, an overproduction of capital goods, a slowdown in growth of consumer demand relative to production, a squeeze on profits, or the inability of banks and other financial institutions to keep on expanding credit—any or all of these factors can contribute to the end of a boom and thus start the economy on a downward course. At that point, the fact that debt has been layered upon debt leads to a domino effect, as debtors scramble to collect funds to pay off pressing claims by lenders. Finance therefore acts as an accelerator of the business cycle, pushing it farther and faster along on the way up and steepening the decline on the way down.

Minsky believes that the role of finance in the United States began to be excessive only during the mid-1960s, and that the absence until then of an unusual acceleration of the cycle due to the functioning of the financial system helped sustain the illusions about the effectiveness of the traditional Keynesian devices. In the first two decades after the Second World War, he suggests, the financial situation of the United States was fairly robust, especially because of favorable cash positions enjoyed by corporations, banks, and consumers resulting from the economics of the war period. By focusing almost entirely on the financial aspects, he overlooks other long-term factors which gave a more solid base to the long wave of prosperity, and he likewise ignores the petering out of the boom-sustaining conditions as well as the resurgence of stagnation tendencies already evident during the mid-1960s.*

While there may be differences of interpretation on the causes, there can be no question about the facts. There was without doubt a significant change in the condition and role of the financial sector of U.S. capitalism in the mid-1960s. The most noteworthy aspect of this was the huge debt explosion that sustained the prosperity phases of the cycles in the late 1960s and early 1970s. Moreover, the nature of the debt explosion, piled on top of a high level of government spending and accumulated government debt, led to the transformation of a fairly strong into an increasingly fragile financial structure. In the last eleven years the United States was faced with three incipient financial crises ("credit crunches," the business press called them): in 1966, 1969-1970, and 1973-1974. At each of these danger points, the alternatives government agencies had to choose between were crystal clear: either permit a "natural"

---

* For historical background, see "The Long-Run Decline in Liquidity," *Monthly Review,* September 1970 and "The Economic Crisis in Historical Perspective," Parts I and II, pp. 55-75 above.

debt deflation along with the likelihood of a major depression and bankruptcies of leading banks, or prop up the financial system. In the absence of a severe depression during which debts are forcefully wiped out or drastically reduced, government rescue measures to prevent collapse of the financial system merely lay the groundwork for still more layers of debt and additional strains during the next economic advance.

The responsibility for trying to prevent a financial collapse falls on the shoulders of the Federal Reserve Board, as the lender of last resort for the banks. What this means is an injection of money to the banks so that they in turn can continue to meet their obligations and overcome the limitations of the "credit crunch." But these steps to prevent a collapse lead, at the same time, to an accelerated increase in the money supply, which continues to feed the fires of inflation. Minsky summarizes these developments as follows:

> The events of the mid-1960s to date have validated the view we have attributed to Keynes that the availability of adequate finance is an essential step in generating and sustaining expansions. The investment boom of the 1960s together with the inventiveness of the financial system in discovering ways to accommodate the demand for finance constitute evidence that the endogenous generation of business cycles remains a basic characteristic of capitalist economies. Because of the efficacy of the Federal Reserve in aborting crises, and because of the high floor to income due to the size of the federal budget, no full-scale debt-deflation process has been triggered. Without a crisis and a debt-deflation process to offset beliefs in the success of speculative ventures, both an upward bias to prices and ever-higher financial layering is induced. (P. 164)

To put it more bluntly, the Keynesians have nothing in their tool-kit to solve the financial instability—or any of the other deep-rooted contradictions—of the system. Despite all the pervasive illusions, the constraints of capitalist economics are such that at this stage there is only a choice between major depression and inflation—and with continuous inflation, even more instability. Ultimately something more, much more, is essential: a society in which production for profit is replaced by production for use, and money and finance are reduced to their proper role as modest accessories to rational planning.